The Way of
ALOHA
Lānaʻi

WHAT READERS ARE SAYING ABOUT

"I just finished your book on Lanai. It really touched me. I would like to meet a man like Manu. It gives me hope to see a 'normal' guy live the truths we know in this gospel! Thank you for the book, and more importantly the spirit I felt conveyed through it. I look forward to the next book."

- Dr. James Gardner

"Just finished reading *The Way of Aloha: Lanai* on the beaches of Maui. I loved it, and I learned so much! Can't wait to read the rest of them! Mahalo, Cameron C. Taylor!!"

- Rachelle Bosh

"Thanks for the book. I read it in one sitting. It was very well written and thoroughly enjoyable. Not being LDS I found it very interesting to learn about that part of the LDS culture. Made me want to go back to Hawaii. Great job."

- Marque Roybal

"Inspiring and heartwarming."

- William Munn

"The author wrote in such a way that I felt like I was there experiencing the emotions as he did. My spirit connected to what he learned in his experiences, and I am happy that he shared the insights and lessons learned."

- Marty Hardy

THE WAY OF ALOHA: LĀNA'I

"This book has inspired me to view the Bible spoken and read differently. So many meanings from the same words. Interesting."

- Cheryl Halbrooks

"I finished *The Way of Aloha: Lanai* in two days because you had me so interested in it. Manu's stories were outstanding—very detailed and moving. I have never been to Hawaii, but have always wanted to go. Your descriptions of the islands reinforced that. And now I don't want to go as just a tourist, but to see it more as a spiritual experience."

- William Croyle

"I absolutely loved the book. Thanks for a great, inspirational story. I am going to read it with my family now."

- Rick Tompot

"I opened your new book and didn't stop until I was done. Your book brought something I needed tonight. Thank you."

- Dr. Bob Sawicki

"I loved the quotes and stories, but the thing I enjoyed most was how *The Way of Aloha* made me feel. I felt peace, love, and a greater understanding of the reality of the Atonement of Jesus Christ. It has blessed my life.

Thank you, Cameron!"

- Jane Charchenko

The Way of
ALOHA
Lāna‘i

CAMERON C. TAYLOR

Other Books by Cameron C. Taylor

8 Attributes of Great Achievers

8 Attributes of Great Achievers, Volume II

Preserve, Protect, & Defend

Does Your Bag Have Holes? 24 Truths That Lead to Financial and Spiritual Freedom

Twelve Paradoxes of the Gospel

8 Steps to Lasting Excellence

Author's Website

www.CameronCTaylor.com

Library of Congress Control Number: 2016918567
ISBN-13: 978-0-9796861-6-0
Printed in the United States of America

Dedicated to the Lord Jesus Christ.
He who is always mindful of the one.

Dedicated to Manu Delbert Tuitupou.
The inspiration for the first name of the character Manu Nāpela.

Dedicated to Jonathan Nāpela.
The inspiration for the last name of the character Manu Nāpela.

Dedicated to Paula Jo Taylor.
The woman who is my inspiration.

Contents

Preface	11
Hawaiian Pronunciation Guide	13
Chapter 1: The Mission Call	14
Chapter 2: Banished to Lāna'i	24
Chapter 3: Our First Lesson	30
Chapter 4: The Naha Fishponds	48
Chapter 5: Halulu Heiau	68
Chapter 6: Garden of the Gods	82
Chapter 7: Hulopo'e Beach	102
Chapter 8: Keōmoku Church	120
Chapter 9: Lāna'i Community Cemetery	138
Chapter 10: Final Week in Lāna'i	148
Epilogue	161
Acknowledgments	163
About the Author	165
Endnotes	167

PREFACE

Last year, I had the impression it was time to write another book. I prayed and contemplated on what to write and how it should be written. I had the impression that I needed to go alone to the mountains to begin the book. I told my wife of the impression and of the mountain cabin I had found for rent in Island Park, Idaho. She quickly agreed that I should go. As I arrived at the cabin, I prayed for the gifts of the Spirit, including the gift of storytelling and the gift of writing. This book is the result of a week in the mountains and many months of work after returning home.

I served as a full-time missionary in the Hawaiʻi Honolulu Mission from 1994 to 1996. Most of this book is set on the island of Lānaʻi, where I served for three months at the beginning of 1996.

Manu Nāpela is a fictional character; however, the principles and stories he shares are true. Manu represents the wisdom and experiences of several people. The other names, places, and accounts throughout the book are factual and are from my missionary journals and memories.

Enjoy the book!

Cameron C. Taylor

HAWAIIAN PRONUNCIATION GUIDE

The Hawaiian alphabet consists of thirteen letters:

Five vowels (a, e, i, o, u)

Eight consonants (h, k, l, m, n, p, w, ʻokina)

The ʻokina is a reversed apostrophe used as a glottal stop

Vowel Pronunciations:

"a" is pronounced like "a" in father

"e" is pronounced like "ey" in they

"i" is pronounced like "ee" in see

"o" is pronounced like "o" in no

"u" is pronounced like "oo" in too

"ai" or "ae" is pronounced like the "i" in ride

"ao" is pronounced like the "ow" in how

"au" is pronounced like the "ou" in loud

"ei" is pronounced as the "ei" in eight

"oi" or "oe" is pronounced like the "oy" in boy

"ou" is pronounced like the "ow" in bowl

"ui" is pronounced like the "ooey" in gooey

"eu" is pronounced: eh-(y)oo

"iu" is pronounced: ee-(y)oo

CHAPTER 1

THE MISSION CALL

"There is not a university in this world that can teach you what you learn on a full-time mission."[1]

- President Howard W. Hunter

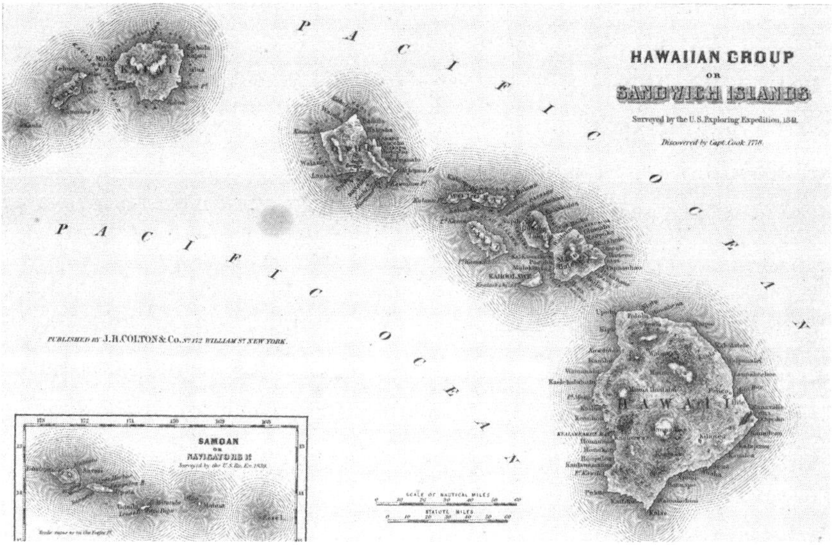

I held a 9 x12 envelope from church headquarters in my hands. My four brothers, sister, and parents sat in a circle in our small living room, waiting anxiously to know where the Lord had called me to serve. I tore open the envelope and, with the letter from President Howard W. Hunter in hand, began to read: "Dear Elder Cameron Taylor, you are hereby called to serve as a missionary of The Church of Jesus Christ of Latter-day Saints. You are assigned to labor in the Hawai'i Honolulu Mission."

My older brother quickly retorted, "Where are you really going?"

I'm one who likes to joke a lot, so I knew they'd need to see to believe. I handed the letter to my brother. "That's not a mission. That's a vacation," he said with a bit of resentment as he read. Then he passed the letter around the circle.

"You must've done something right in the preexistence because you certainly didn't do anything here to deserve this," another brother declared.

I laughed off the comments, but secretly agreed. I didn't know what I'd done to deserve such a blessing.

A few months later, on September 14, 1994, I reported to the Missionary Training Center (MTC) in Provo, Utah. After a quick three weeks there, it was time to catch a flight to Honolulu. It was a long day of travel that began very early; but I gained four hours during the flight, so it was still afternoon when I arrived. I was the only elder entering the mission that month. As I walked to the baggage claim area, I was greeted with a warm "Aloha" and a beautiful flower lei from the assistants to the president.

"I hope you have room for my golf clubs in the car!" I announced, a grin on my face. My smile was met with a stern look. It was clear my humor wasn't appreciated by my current company.

The assistants, Elder Osterhout and Elder Hale, put me to work immediately. As we entered the city, they stopped the car and said it was time to do some tracting. The three of us approached the front door of a small home. As I rang the doorbell, the two assistants stepped back. A Japanese woman emerged, scrutinizing the stranger who stood before her. My mind went blank and my tongue froze. I stood there silently, looking at her. I expected my companions to come to my rescue, but to my horror, they remained several steps away, refusing to come to my aid. After several seconds of silence, the woman closed the door. I humbly turned and walked toward the assistants.

"Elder Taylor, you have to say something," Elder Osterhout said. "Let's try another door."

As we walked up to another home, I mentally prepared myself for my next interaction with a stranger. This time, a man opened the door.

"Do you know why it's important to be quiet in church?" I asked him.

"I'm not sure," the man replied, puzzled.

"Because people are sleeping," I said with a smile.

The man laughed and I introduced myself as Elder Taylor with The Church of Jesus Christ of Latter-day Saints. He said he wasn't interested and closed the door.

As I turned, Elder Hale said, "I've never heard that door approach."

"I've found that humor and laughter are a powerful way to break down barriers and build friendships," I said.

"I don't think the mission president will approve of that approach," he responded. "We'll work on your door approaches later. We need to head to the mission home so you can meet the mission president and his wife. But don't worry. You'll get to do plenty of tracting over the next 730 days."

As we traveled, I scanned the magnificent scenery surrounding me with eager eyes. I noticed tiny houses clumped closely together.

"Residential land is a scarce commodity around here," said Elder Osterhout, following my gaze out the car window. "Honolulu is a sixty-eight-square-mile city with nearly six thousand people living in each square mile. Nearly one million live in Honolulu County. That's a lot of potential investigators."

I nodded vaguely, my eyes still focused on the houses rushing by. Fifteen minutes later, we pulled into the driveway of a pretty home in a nice neighborhood. The driveway and yard were small but well kept.

We made the short walk to the door and were greeted with an "Aloha" and hug from President Fairbourn. After removing our shoes in the entryway, President Fairbourn took us into the dining room adjacent to the kitchen. Sister Fairbourn stopped her work to come and greet us. Approaching me first, she warmly said, "Aloha," and gave me a loving embrace.

I come from a family of non-huggers. I'd already set a record for most hugs in a day after only being on the island a few hours. The frequent hugging was going to take some adjustment on my part.

After sharing a meal with President and Sister Fairbourn, I spent the night with the assistants at their apartment. The following morning, President Fairbourn drove me to the north shore of O'ahu to the city of Laie, for my first missionary assignment. It was a unique opportunity to spend an hour alone with the missionary president as we drove along the Kamehameha Highway. The scenery was magnificent, with the beach and ocean on the right and the lush green mountains and waterfalls to the left.

"Elder Taylor, President Hunter recently visited our mission and in his remarks he said, 'There is not a university in this world that can teach you what you learn on a full-time mission.' You may get vocational training at a university, but the most important education comes in knowing and living the gospel of Jesus Christ," he told me. "As you begin your service as a full-time disciple and minister of the Lord Jesus Christ, I would like to illustrate to you the influence we have on others."

He went on to tell me the story of a young girl he'd met at a youth conference.

Sally was raised by a single mom because of divorce. When she was nine years old, she came to understand that her mom was an alcoholic. She asked her mom if she could live with her dad. Sally's mom wasn't sure where he was but said she thought she could find him. When she found him, Sally went to live with him. But she was deeply saddened as she quickly learned that her dad was also an alcoholic.

By the time Sally entered high school, she was very discouraged and disgusted with life. During her sophomore year, she made friends with a girl named Kristy, who was in her biology class. One Friday, Kristy invited her home for a slumber party. Sally wasn't sure she wanted to go and didn't know what to expect. There were eight other girls at the party. They ate pizza, laughed, and giggled all night long. Sally had a wonderful time and hoped Kristy would invite her again. And she did. Sally had many fun slumber parties at Kristy's home, and over time, Kristy's family began to ask Sally to stay for the whole weekend. Sally dreaded when Monday would come because she had to return home. Kristy and Sally became best friends.

A few days before Sally's birthday, Kristy told her she had a very special birthday present for her. Sally was excited to receive the present, so she went to school early. She waited by Kristy's locker for her to arrive. When Kristy arrived, she said hello, placed her lunch in her locker, and they parted ways to their different classes. Kristy didn't even mention Sally's birthday. Sally was upset, thinking her best friend had forgotten. She avoided Kristy during lunch and biology class. After school, Sally saw Kristy at her locker, and she couldn't be silent any longer. With a bit of anger and sadness in her voice, Sally said, "You forgot my birthday." Kristy quickly answered, "No, I haven't," as she reached into her locker and pulled out the bag Sally had assumed was her lunch. "I wanted to give you your gift after school when we could be alone."

The girls went under a secluded tree near the school. Kristy pulled a wrapped present out of the paper bag and asked Sally to open it. She unwrapped the gift to find a *Book of Mormon*. As Sally opened the book, she saw on the inside cover a picture of Kristy smiling, along with her written testimony. As Sally looked at the book, Kristy said, "This book means a lot to me, and I wanted to share it with you because you mean a lot to me. I love you!"

It was the first time that Sally could remember hearing those words. She was very grateful for her gift, her friendship, and her love. She went home that Tuesday and began reading. Sally was engrossed in the book and read deep into the night. During class, she snuck the book inside her textbooks so she could continue reading. By Friday, Sally had completed the *Book of Mormon*. When she went to stay at Kristy's home for the weekend, she was excited to talk to them about what she'd read and learned. That weekend, Sally asked Kristy's father if he would baptize her. He contacted Sally's parents to get permission to do so. In the meetings with them, he learned they didn't care what their daughter did and that neither of them wanted her.

President Fairbourn interjected his own words with tears in his eyes, "I couldn't believe what she was telling me. Here was this beautiful girl, and her family didn't want her. She was baptized by

Brother Hansen, and the Hansens began the process of adopting her. She became a part of the Hansen family and was sealed to them in the temple. She concluded her story to me by pointing to Kristy, who was standing beside her. With tears running down her cheeks, she said, 'She is my sister, and I love her.'"

President Fairbourn noticed me wiping at my eyes. "Elder Taylor," he went on, his gaze focused on the road in front of us. "There are many people throughout the islands who feel that no one loves them. That no one wants them. That they don't have a family. You carry with you a message of family. The family of the Lord Jesus Christ. Christ wants them in His family. He loves them more than they can comprehend. He wants to say to them, 'I am your brother and I love you.' Elder Taylor, that is why you are here. To share with these wonderful people of Hawai'i the joys that come from being a part of a family—the family of Jesus Christ. You bring the message of redemption, hope, and forgiveness. No matter the challenges and tragedies in their past, with Christ, they have a beautiful future."

President Fairbourn pointed out his window to a building on our left. "There is the Polynesian Cultural Center (PCC). We are getting close to your apartment. As you continue to look to the left, you will see BYU–Hawai'i and the temple."

The car slowed as we approached a road perpendicular to Kamehameha Highway, and the Laie Hawai'i Temple came into view. It sat about a half-mile away, at the base of a beautiful, lush, green mountain backdrop. The pure white bricks of the angular temple, made from crushed lava rocks and reinforced concrete, were framed by palm trees lining the street. I'd seen many pictures of the temple, but a photo cannot fully capture the beauty and spirit of this building and its surroundings. The feeling of peace and power was majestic; the feeling was made more powerful by the Spirit that had filled the car as President Fairbourn shared Sally's story.

We continued about another half-mile before President Fairbourn pulled in front of a small apartment just off the highway, across from Hukilau Beach. I later learned the beach was a filming location for portions of the famous church movie, *Johnny Lingo.*

"Welcome to Laie, Elder Taylor. It is time to get to work," President Fairbourn said with a smile.

CHAPTER 2

BANISHED TO LĀNA'I

"I'll answer, dear Lord, with my hand in thine: I'll go where you want me to go."[2]

- Mary Brown

I served in Laie for six months, until I was transferred to serve as the zone leader of the Mililani zone. The Mililani zone covered the west side of the north shore and the central part of O‘ahu. After five months in Mililani, I was transferred to serve as the zone leader in the Honolulu West area. While in Honolulu West, I was assigned to minister on the Pearl Harbor Naval Base. During my fourth month as the Honolulu West zone leader, the phone rang at the appointed time for transfers. I had my notebook and pen ready to write. After giving me several transfers, the assistant to the president paused and said, "I have one last transfer. Elder Taylor, you are going to Lāna‘i."

I was happy to serve wherever the Lord wanted me to go, but I was puzzled by the assignment. Lāna‘i was where the mission president sent problem missionaries. Being sent to Lāna‘i was viewed by everyone in the mission as a punishment. Elders who were sent there were said to be "banished."

I lived with five other elders in a house in the town of Aiea, outside of Honolulu. My roommates and fellow elders laughed when they heard about my new assignment.

"What did you do, Elder Taylor?" asked Elder Vergara. "Do you have a girlfriend we don't know about?"

"How does it feel to be banished?" asked Elder Soriano with a smile.

I laughed at their teasing, despite the concern welling up inside me. Why was I being sent away? Had I made a mistake?

On transfer day, I got to meet with the mission president before my flight to Lāna'i. President Anderson was new to the islands, having taken over for President Fairbourn five months earlier. After we settled into our chairs, I asked, "Why are you sending me to Lāna'i? Have I done something wrong?"

The mission president chuckled. "No. You haven't done anything wrong. In fact, you've done something right. I know President Fairbourn used Lāna'i as a place of banishment, but that isn't the case here. I've spent a lot of time praying about Lāna'i. There has not been a single convert baptism on the island in seven years. The two elders who are on Lāna'i now tell me, in their letters, that there is no missionary work to be done."

President Anderson sighed and rubbed his eyes before continuing. "President Fairbourn never visited the island and neither have I. No assistant to the president or zone leader has been to Lāna'i. I've thought, if there is no missionary work to be done, maybe it's time to close the area and move the two elders assigned to Lāna‘i somewhere else. As I prayed about what to do, the Lord told me to call Elder Taylor to Lāna‘i, and so I did. I know Lāna‘i is where the Lord wants you to be." He smiled at my look of surprise and patted my knee. "I look forward to hearing your reports."

Although our meeting was brief, it was exactly what I needed to hear. I was excited for a new challenge and adventure, and for an opportunity to get away from the concrete jungle and traffic of Honolulu to serve in a new piece of the Lord's island vineyard. I would also be going back to a bicycle, which was my preferred method of travel. I found it easier to connect with people—and with the spirit and power of the island—while on a bicycle.

I was dropped off at the Honolulu airport with the other elders who were transferring to the outer islands. The majority of the missionaries served on the island of O‘ahu, as it contains seventy percent of Hawaii's population. I, on the other hand, would be going from serving in a town with nearly one million people to an island with a total population of around 3,000. I travelled alone, as I was the only elder going to Lāna‘i. I had my one-way tickets from Honolulu to Maui and Maui to Lāna‘i. The flight was a quick trip on two small commuter planes with seats for eight.

I landed on the tiny one-runway airport, feeling every jerk and shake of the tiny plane as it landed on the rugged cement below. In the small terminal, I was met by my new companion, Elder Balane, and a member of the Lāna‘i branch, Stanley Oshima. Stanley took us from the airport to the missionary quarters at the branch building.

The missionary quarters consisted of a small studio apartment attached to the church. There were two twin beds with an aisle barely wide enough for a person to walk between them, a sparse kitchen area, and a tiny bathroom. There was no heating or air conditioning. Lāna'i City was in the mountains, so it could get below sixty degrees at night, which is very cold for Hawai'i. When the nights grew cold, we turned on the oven and left the oven door open to heat the apartment. I would often joke with Elder Balane, "Do you want me to set the thermostat to 350 or 400 degrees?"

Lāna'i is the smallest inhabited island in Hawai'i, measuring seventeen miles long and thirteen miles wide. It was once the home of the world's largest pineapple plantation. Lāna'i City was built in the 1920s to house and serve the plantation workers. Between the late 1980s and early 1990s, Lāna'i was transitioning out of the pineapple business and into the resort business. Two resorts were built on the island. The Lodge at Kō'ele opened in 1990 and the Mānele Bay Resort opened in 1991. In October, 1992, the final harvest of pineapple on Lāna'i took place. One month later, on November 14, a Pau Hana (end of work) gathering was held in Dole Park to commemorate the close of the pineapple era. The major employer of the island had officially shifted from the plantation to the resorts.

Lāna'i City was an easy town to travel around on a bike. There are no traffic lights and only a few miles of paved roads. I would soon discover that missionaries were part of the Lāna'i family, and my companion and I were warmly greeted and waved to as we rode our bikes through the city.

CHAPTER 3

OUR FIRST LESSON

"The best way to obtain truth and wisdom is not to ask it from books, but to go to God in prayer, and obtain divine teaching."

- Joseph Smith

Although I didn't have fifty meal appointments each week like in my first area, the people of Lāna'i took great care of us. The Lāna'i branch consisted of five active families, and they fed us every week. The dinner schedule was as follows: the Nāpela family on Monday, the Kawasaki family on Tuesday, the Oshima family on Thursday, the Bulaoat family on Friday, and the Poulson family on Saturday. Each Sunday, there was a potluck at the church following the block of meetings. It was joyous to be in the homes of these faithful saints each week.

On Wednesdays, we were fed by the Elans. They were a young couple who weren't members of the church, but they loved feeding the missionaries. At my first dinner appointment, the Elans asked what I liked to eat. I told them I loved jumbo prawns. The next week, there was a huge pyramid of freshly caught prawns. We ate and ate and ate prawns until the pile was gone. Uncle Elan caught fresh prawns for us every week, and I so looked forward to Wednesday nights. It was a beautiful sight to walk into their home and see the tower of prawns that filled their small table.

Looking back, I'm surprised how well I was treated as a missionary because my physical appearance was quite comical. For starters, I looked like I was fourteen years old. My usual attire consisted of a wrinkly white shirt, worn slacks that should've been replaced months ago, a fifty-cent used tie stained with food, and a backpack that was large enough for a week-long hiking trip. My hair always looked like it hadn't been combed in days (the consequence of riding around with a bicycle helmet), and one pant leg was often tucked into my sock so it wouldn't get caught in my bicycle chain. Although I was inexperienced, unsophisticated, and awkward, I cherished these days filled with much joy and many wonderful memories. I did my best to serve the Lord, lift others, and share a message I loved.

Our P-day—a day when missionaries take time to prepare for the week ahead—was on Mondays. I spent my first P-day in Lāna'i, unpacking, writing a few letters, and doing some grocery shopping. I'd never had to buy food in my other areas, so my first visit to the Lāna'i grocery store was a tremendous shock. It wasn't just that I had to buy my own food for the first time since arriving in Hawai'i. It was that a box of Cheerios and a gallon of milk cost me $16.

For lunch that same day, Elder Balane introduced me to a way to keep our costs down—the avocado sandwich. There was an avocado tree at the church, so we had free access to the tropical fruit. We mashed them up, added some sugar, and spread the mixture on a piece of bread for a tasty sandwich. However, by five o'clock, I was starving again. I was used to eating six large meals a day. I was very much looking forward to our dinner appointment with the Nāpela family. We took the short, five-minute bike ride to their home and arrived several minutes early, anxious to eat.

As we parked our bikes, I could smell a wonderful aroma coming from their home. My mouth watered and my stomach growled. I knew I was in for a great Hawaiian meal that would be much more filling than the bowl of cereal I'd eaten for breakfast and the avocado sandwich I'd had for lunch. Brother Nāpela answered the door in cargo shorts and an Aloha shirt. He greeted us with a warm "Aloha" before directing us to the dining room. The family was already gathered, and we took our places at the table. I was excited to see they were ready to eat, even though we were a few minutes early.

Brother Nāpela offered the prayer. I'd been in the islands for over a year and this was the first time I heard someone bless the food in Hawaiian. I'd heard prayers in Samoan and Tongan, but there were not many left on the islands who spoke Hawaiian. As he said the prayer, I was filled with the Spirit in great fashion, even though I didn't understand anything he was saying. He was not singing, but the words felt like a wonderful song of praise and thanksgiving as the beautiful rhythmic prayer fell from his tongue with passion and love. I knew there was something special about Brother Nāpela.

The prayer ended and it was time to eat. Before me was a familiar scene of a Polynesian feast, larger than a mainland Thanksgiving. The table was filled with kalua pork, teriyaki chicken, and plenty of rice.

I've never been described as one who is large in stature. At times, it felt overwhelming to be surrounded by the Polynesians. Next to my 150-pound frame, they seemed like giants. Brother Nāpela was a large man. He was well over six feet tall and weighed somewhere in the neighborhood of three hundred pounds.

I piled my plate high with food and began to eat. I didn't participate much in the conversation while I worked to fill my empty stomach.

As I began dishing up seconds, I asked, "Brother Nāpela, what do you do for work?"

"I teach at the Lāna'i High and Elementary school. And please call me Manu."

"Okay," I said, setting my now full plate in front of me and eagerly shoveling a bite of pork into my mouth. "What subject do you teach?"

"I teach Hawaiian language and history."

"Sounds very interesting. How many students are at the school?" I asked.

"There are around six hundred students in all the grades, kindergarten to twelfth. We have a low teacher to student ratio, which is nice," he said. "We have one teacher for every fifteen students."

"How many total people live on the island?" I asked.

Manu seemed to enjoy my line of questioning, leaning back in his chair as he considered his answer. "There are around three thousand, with pretty much everyone living in Lāna'i City. It's a nice, small community. Everyone here knows the missionaries. You'll be like part of the family. In fact, the missionaries are often called to serve as substitute teachers at the school."

He chuckled when I looked at my companion in surprise.

"It's true. I've already been a substitute teacher several times. We also volunteer at the school on Thursdays as a part of the reading program. They have the missionaries read books to the elementary children. Maybe one of these weeks, they'll have us read them Brother Nāpela's books."

Manu laughed. "I don't think that will ever happen. My books aren't interesting enough for the elementary children."

Sister Nāpela chimed in. "Manu will never say so, but he's considered one of the world's experts on ancient Hawaiian culture, history, and language."

"I'm very interested in learning about the Hawaiian culture and language," I said, excited to be sitting across from an expert. "Would you be willing to teach us? I've asked about Hawaiian history in my other areas and no one seems to know much."

"Do you really want to learn?" Manu asked.

"Absolutely," Elder Balane and I answered in unison.

"Alright then. We can't detract from your important work as full-time missionaries, so this will have to be done on your P-days. Are you okay with that?" Manu asked.

Elder Balane and I nodded.

"Well, since today is your P-day, are you ready for your first experience?" Manu asked.

"Sure," Elder Balane said as I nodded with excitement.

Manu stood from his chair and announced, "Then let's get in the car. We don't want to miss it."

"Miss what?" I asked.

"You'll see. Let's go." He paused on his way out the door to slip on a pair of flip-flops.

Elder Balane and I stopped to shove our feet into our own shoes, with far less grace, and followed Manu to his truck. As we buckled our seat belts, I repeated my earlier question, "Where are we going?"

"I already told you. You will see. Do you like to laugh?"

"Well, of course," I answered.

"Laughter is a very important part of Hawaiian life," he said as he started the truck and pulled away from his house. "Ancient Hawaiians understood that laughter is one of the greatest of all emotions and is a pure form of communication with God. Direct communion with God is experienced with joyous laughter. Life should be filled with joy and laughter."

I pulled out the small notebook I always kept in my back pocket so I could take notes. "Is this our first lesson?"

Manu laughed. "You're used to learning in the mainland with lectures and taking notes. I wasn't giving you information to write down. I was going to tell you a story. Are you ready?"

"Sure," I replied, hesitating with the notebook in my lap. Should I put the notebook away? What if he said something I needed to write down?

Manu's eyes rested on the notebook in my lap for a moment before he shook his head and smiled, turning his eyes back to the road in front of us. "My wife was preparing pancakes for two of our sons when they were age five and three," he said. "The boys began to argue over who would get the first pancake. Their mother saw the opportunity for a moral lesson and said, 'If Jesus were sitting here,

He would say, 'Let my brother have the first pancake. I can wait.' Following my wife's comment, my oldest son turned to his younger brother and said, 'You be Jesus!'"

Elder Balane and I laughed. Manu joined in. His jolly Polynesian laugh was contagious, which made us laugh even more. After our laughing subsided, Manu said, "The ancient Hawaiian word for laughter means to lift and expand. Laughter lifts your spirit and heals your body. Laughter expands your ability to connect with God and feel His presence. You fulfill the measure of your creation when your life is filled with joy. God is pleased when He sees you laughing, as laughter is evidence that you are happy. Happiness is the purpose of your creation."

I jotted down Manu's anecdote in my notebook as he continued. "The ancient Hawaiians didn't teach in the sterile setting of a classroom. They taught with story, dance, song, and experience. Elder Taylor, you need to put your notebook away. You must learn the ways of the ancient Hawaiians with your heart, not with a pen. The heart learns by doing."

"How will I remember what you teach if I don't write it down?" I asked.

"What I am going to teach you is a way of life, not a list of facts," he chided gently. "The only way an idea or principle can truly be known and remembered is for it to become a part of the way you live. You'll learn much more with your heart than with your mind."

I didn't fully comprehend what he was saying but I put the notebook away as directed.

"The ancient Hawaiians had no written language and kept no

written records, yet they had a detailed genealogy, a large reservoir of divine truth, and a way of life that could be called Zion," Manu said. "Their genealogy, truth, and way of life were passed from generation to generation through ho'o ka'ao. Have you heard the phrase, 'Let's talk story?'"

"Sure," I answered. "I thought it was a weird phrase at first, but quickly learned that Hawaiians loved to tell and hear stories."

Manu nodded. "The modern phrase, 'Let's talk story' has its origins in ho'o ka'ao, which is the art of storytelling. As did the Master teacher Jesus Christ, the Hawaiians share wisdom through stories."

As Manu was talking, the road became extremely rough. In fact, I don't think you could call what we were on a road or even a dirt trail. It was more like a rugged path of rocks and ruts. I tried to brace myself against the seat and passenger door but it didn't make much difference. We bounced in Manu's four-wheel-drive truck with our heads and shoulders swinging side to side and our teeth rattling.

"Have you taken us off road?" I asked.

Manu laughed. "No, this is the road. It's not easy to get to Polihua Beach, but well worth the effort. This road reminds me of the quote by Thomas Paine, 'What we obtain too cheap, we esteem too lightly. 'Tis dearness only that gives everything its value. Heaven knows how to put a proper price upon its goods.'[3] I believe the price to get to Polihua Beach should be a high price." He paused and looked at me, as if expecting me to pull my notebook back out. He smiled when I didn't. "Once you've experienced it, you will know why I say this."

After thirty minutes of treacherous terrain and tree branches tapping an unsteady rhythm as they hit the sides of the truck, we came to the end of the road. We emerged from the trees to a spectacular view of an isolated beach, vast ocean, and the sight of Moloka'i across the channel. The few seconds of initial awe as I took in the scene were well worth the bumpy ride. There are places that cannot be fully captured with words or even with a camera, and this was one of those places. The panoramic views, untouched beauty, and peaceful serenity were celestial.

Manu parked his truck and instructed us to take off our shoes and socks so we could feel the sand between our toes as we walked. I'd seen many beautiful beaches throughout my service in Hawai'i, but this one stood alone in its majestic beauty. I've been to dozens of beaches throughout the world since serving in Hawai'i, and this is still the most beautiful one I've ever seen. I scanned the two miles of gorgeous sand and endless skyscape. There was not another person in sight. For a moment, I felt as if I were the only person on the planet; like it was just me, God, and His wondrous creations.

The vastness of the beach extended from the ocean into the trees lining the beach, a burst of brilliant green against a blue sky. We followed Manu in silence, drinking in the soothing sounds of the ocean waves and the wind brushing through the trees. The distant smell of salt water wafted to me on the wind. My soul was invigorated as I inhaled the pure, crisp air that surrounded us.

It was nearing sunset as we found a comfortable place to sit on the beach. After a few moments of silence, Manu spoke, his voice filling the soothing silence like a warm fire.

"Let's talk story," he said as he pulled a few folded papers from his pocket. "President David O. McKay visited the islands of Samoa in 1921 and recorded in his journal under the header 'A Beautiful Vision' the following: 'We sailed all day on the smoothest sea of our entire trip. Towards evening, the reflection of the afterglow of a beautiful sunset was most splendid! The sky was tinged with pink, and the clouds lingering around the horizon were fringed with various hues of crimson and orange, while the heavy cloud farther to the west was somber purple and black. These various colors cast varying shadows on the peaceful surface of the water. Those from the cloud were long and dark, those from the crimson-tinged sky, clear but rose-tinted and fading into a faint pink that merged into the clear blue of the ocean. Gradually, the shadows became deeper and heavier, and then all merged into a beautiful calm twilight that made the sea look like a great mirror upon which fell the faint light of the crescent moon!

"'Pondering still upon this beautiful scene, I lay in my berth at ten o'clock that night, and thought to myself: Charming as it is, it doesn't stir my soul with emotion as do the innocent lives of children, and the sublime characters of loved ones and friends. Their beauty, unselfishness, and heroism are, after all, the most glorious!

"'I then fell asleep, and beheld in vision something infinitely sublime. In the distance, I beheld a beautiful white city. Though far away, yet I seemed to realize that trees with luscious fruit, shrubbery with gorgeously-tinted leaves, and flowers in perfect bloom abounded everywhere. The clear sky above seemed to reflect these beautiful shades of color. I then saw a great concourse of people approaching the city. Each one wore a white flowing robe, and a white headdress.

Instantly my attention seemed centered upon their Leader, and though I could see only the profile of his features and his body, I recognized Him at once as my Savior! The tint and radiance of His countenance were glorious to behold! There was a peace about Him which seemed sublime—it was divine!

"'The city, I understood, was His. It was the City Eternal; and the people following Him were to abide there in peace and eternal happiness. But who were they? As if the Savior read my thoughts, He answered by pointing to a semicircle that then appeared above them, and on which were written in gold the words: 'These Are They Who Have Overcome The World—Who Have Truly Been Born Again!' When I awoke, it was breaking day.'"[4]

The Spirit joined us there, unrestrained. We were wrapped in the love and peace of the Savior as tears trickled down our cheeks. We sat basking in the Spirit as the sun hit the horizon. The three of us gazed outward, watching the setting sun and the brilliant colors radiate throughout the sky. It was as if time stood still and, for a moment, a piece of Heaven had come to earth. The downward motion of the sun appeared to accelerate as the uppermost portions disappeared behind the horizon. Shades of purple, pink, orange, and yellow danced through the clouds.

Manu spoke, "A sunset is like watching God as He paints on His heavenly canvas. A clear reminder of the immensity of God's power, creations, and grace."

Manu paused, letting the silence carry his words deep into our hearts.

"President McKay's story illustrates a pattern for divine

learning," he said after a moment. "I've seen this vision shared in various articles and books, and oftentimes, only the dream is shared with the previous description of nature excluded. I believe there is an important reason why President McKay included the details of the sunset. President McKay's experience with God in nature is a part of 'The Beautiful Vision' and is part of the revelation he received. Nature helps us connect with God. Nature helps us hear God speaking to us. The ancient Hawaiians had a deep connection to God and His creations. I believe one of the reasons people are drawn to Hawai'i is because, while they are surrounded by the beauty of God's creations, they also increase their connection with God."

Elder Balane and I nodded in agreement, but neither of us spoke.

"There is a Hawaiian phrase *aloha 'āina*," Manu said. "The literal translation is 'love of the land,' but as with all Hawaiian words, the definition cannot be captured with a few words of translation. The phrase *aloha 'āina* is a connection with God and His creations. It's the land that nourishes our body and spirit. Nature is a great gift from our Creator and is much more than physical objects. 'Āina is filled with mana (spiritual power), spirit, and breath (life). Land is sacred. Each island of Hawai'i has a unique voice. The 'āina whispers the ancient truths of Aloha. This 'āina makes us proud to live here and is one of the reasons people are drawn here to visit."

"I agree that the land speaks," I said, eager to dig deeper into the concepts Manu was sharing. "When I landed on Lāna'i last week and stepped off the plane, I was overwhelmed with a feeling of peace and a profound feeling of unity. I didn't quite know how to record the experience. I wrote in my journal that it felt like the island was speaking to me."

Manu smiled and he placed his hand on my back. "Yes, the land speaks. Once you experience 'āina, you know it is much more than the English word 'land.' 'Āina is connected to God, and God is connected to 'āina. Understanding the principles of 'āina will help you receive revelation. I'm not your teacher. I'm simply a facilitator for divine instruction. You can learn more in a few minutes from a direct revelation than you can from a hundred books. Joseph Smith taught, 'The best way to obtain truth and wisdom is not to ask it from books, but to go to God in prayer and obtain divine teaching.'"[5]

Manu let that truth sink in for a moment. "I'm obviously a big advocate of books," he said. "I've written a half a dozen of them; but true learning comes from above. Books should be used as a catalyst for divine teaching, not an end in and of themselves. I think this is what the Lord meant when He said, 'Seek ye out of the best books words of wisdom, seek learning even by study and, also by faith.'[6] The study of books should be a catalyst for learning by faith and direct revelation. We must each learn for ourselves and not simply rely on the learning of others. I think this is what Albert Einstein meant when he said, 'Reading, after a certain age, diverts the mind too much from its creative pursuits. Any man who reads too much and uses his own brain too little falls into lazy habits of thinking.'"[7]

Manu turned to Elder Balane, who'd been staring out at the sunset quietly. "What are your thoughts?"

Elder Balane tilted his head as he tried to gather his thoughts. "We often learn more by what we feel than by what we hear," he said.

"I'll always remember how I feel right now, sitting on this beach. While I can't put my feelings into words, I can say that by what I felt, I know there is a God in Heaven, I know He loves me more than I can comprehend, and I know that Jesus is the leader of the divine city that awaits us; and I'm anxious to be united with Him. This scripture also comes to mind: 'All things denote there is a God; yea, even the earth, and all things that are upon the face of it, yea, and its motion, yea, and also all the planets which move in their regular form do witness that there is a Supreme Creator.'"[8]

Elder Balane's observation felt like a good thought to end on and we all seemed to understand this without having to speak it aloud. Although Polihua Beach was a place we didn't want to leave, we all quietly stood and made our way back to Manu's truck.

It felt like a once-in-a-lifetime opportunity, and it may have been. I haven't returned to Lāna'i since leaving, but one day I plan to go back with my family and take them to this sacred place.

We cleaned the sand from our feet and climbed into the truck. As we drove back through the trees and over the ruts and rocks, I felt calmer than I had on the journey in. The jostling didn't bother me. My soul was at peace.

"The islands of Hawai'i are filled with natural wonders and great beauty," Manu said, breaking the silence a few minutes into our drive. "Even greater beauty is found in the Hawaiian way of life. In my extensive study of modern and ancient civilizations, the happiest place on earth is found in the villages of ancient Hawai'i. Paradise is not a location. It's a way of life. The spirit of Aloha and the joy of living are not dependent on *where* you live, but on *how* you live. A life of Aloha can be experienced by anyone, anytime, and anywhere by adhering to the beliefs, attitudes, and actions that make it so. Wherever you go can be paradise. The inner journey to Aloha is much more powerful and profound than a physical trip to Hawai'i. There is an island paradise inside each of us. You just have to find it."

"A few hours ago, I wouldn't have understood or believed what you just said about Aloha and paradise," Elder Balane said. "But, after this experience. I know it's true."

"There is great mana (spiritual power) in the way of Aloha. A Gallup Poll was conducted that asked the question, 'If money were no object, where would you go on your dream vacation?'" Manu said. "The question used an open-ended format, allowing the respondents to name whatever place came to mind. Hawai'i was the number one response by a significant margin. When I saw these results, I thought, 'There are so many beautiful places in the world, why did they choose Hawai'i?' While Hawai'i is beautiful, it also has a spirit and way of life that is magnetic. People are drawn to the Hawaiian Islands to experience Aloha—a life of peace, joy, and family."

We spent the rest of the drive discussing the unique culture of Hawai'i and the beauty of the islands.

When Manu pulled into his small driveway a half an hour later, I didn't want to get out. I wanted to learn more. We sat in silence for a moment. I was hoping Manu would teach us more, but instead, he opened the driver's side door and climbed out of his truck. "Our time is up for today. I will see you next Monday at three thirty."

Elder Balane and I exited the truck and walked toward our bikes. I looked back at the truck to see it covered in red mud. Our first expedition with Manu was an inspiring adventure, but I had a feeling the best was still to come.

Elder Balane and I made a few quick visits to our investigators and then headed home for the night. Immediately upon entering my room, I grabbed my journal so I could record my experience with Manu. I knew the Lord had placed him in my path as a mentor to increase my discipleship and prepare me for things that were to come.

CHAPTER 4

THE NAHA FISHPONDS

"If there be eyes to see, there will be visions to inspire. If there be ears to hear, there will be revelations to experience. If there be hearts which can understand know this: that the exalting truths of Christ's gospel will no longer be hidden and mysterious."[9]

- President Spencer W. Kimball

Each Thursday, Elder Balane and I had a standing appointment at the school library to read to a group of elementary children. After we finished reading, I decided to see if I could find any of Manu's books. I went to the library catalog and found the call numbers. After a little searching, I located one of his books and pulled it from the shelf with great interest. Turning to the back of the book, I scanned Brother Nāpela's bio and learned he'd graduated from BYU–Hawai'i with a degree in Hawaiian Studies. I continued through the library, found the other books by him and proceeded to check them out. I knew they'd be helpful to form a foundation of the Hawaiian language, history, and culture.

It was a joy to serve among the great people of Lāna'i, and time passed very quickly. Soon, Monday arrived and it was time for our next meeting with Manu. Elder Balane and I hopped onto our bikes for the short ride over to the school, where we'd agreed to meet him. It was another beautiful, sunny day in the mid-seventies with clear blue skies and a light breeze.

Though it was P-day, which allowed for more casual attire, I was dressed in a pair of wrinkled slacks and a white, short-sleeved, button-up shirt. I was enjoying the weather so much, I almost wished we had further to ride as we arrived at Manu's classroom. We entered the room to find Manu at his desk, sorting papers. He was in an outfit similar to what he'd worn when we first met—shorts and a floral print aloha shirt.

As we entered the room, Manu stood up from his desk and greeted us with a strong and lengthy, "A-lo-ha."

Elder Balane and I replied in unison with our best, "A-lo-ha."

Manu gave us hugs, wrapping his arms around our bodies and lifting each of us off the ground in turn.

"Elder Taylor, I noticed that when I hug you, it makes you uncomfortable," Manu said as we walked to his truck.

"Is it that obvious?" I asked, surprised. "I've never liked giving or receiving hugs. However, I've received more hugs over the past year than during the first eighteen years of my life. Although hugs still make me feel uncomfortable, I'm getting better at giving and receiving them."

"Do you have any idea why?" Manu asked me. I paused at the door of the truck and considered his question.

"Well, in my family we didn't hug, so I think part of it is cultural," I said as I slid onto the bench seat. Manu settled behind the wheel as Elder Balane climbed in beside me. "It's not something I'm used to. I think it might also be tied to negative events from my childhood."

Here I paused and sucked in a deep breath. I considered stopping my explanation there but realized I wanted to be completely honest with Manu. He looked at me with warm understanding and I felt safe sharing the whole truth with him.

"I'm just coming to realize that sexual abuse occurred when I was young," I said. "I have occasional flashbacks and memories of the abuse. Several years ago, it was discovered that one of my relatives was a pedophile. As a teenager, I remember getting mad at my parents when they asked if I was abused by this relative. I would answer in a sharp tone—something like, 'I think I would know if I was abused. Why do you keep asking me this?'"

I looked at Elder Balane and Manu, unsure about how they were reacting to my disclosure. They both nodded in understanding and Manu gestured for me to continue.

"My mind had blocked it out, and I had no memory of the abuse," I continued, shrugging. "In fact, I have very little memory of my childhood at all. As a result of the abuse, I have a hard time trusting people, especially those older than me. I have a hard time feeling a connection with or love for others. It's like that part of my heart has been turned off. I know a hug is supposed to be an expression of love, but to me, it feels like awkward sandpaper."

There was a moment of silence as Manu pulled out of the school parking lot. "I am so sorry to hear that," he said, his voice soft. "Sexual abuse is far too common in the United States. I've heard as many as one in five children are sexually abused before they're eighteen."

"Is it really that high?" Elder Balane asked.

"It sure is. So, there are a lot of people dealing with the effects of abuse. Would you mind if I give you another hug?" Manu asked.

"Well, I can tell we are going to be hugging each time we meet, so I guess I had better get used to it." I let out a nervous laugh.

Manu pulled the truck to the side of the road and wrapped his large Hawaiian arms around me, squeezing tightly. "I love you, Elder Taylor," he said.

I considered Manu my friend, and I could feel his concern and love for me. But it still felt awkward and uncomfortable. I couldn't stop my body from tensing up.

While still holding me he said, "The typical response, Elder Taylor, would be, 'I love you, too.'"

Manu held me, waiting for my response. I tried to formulate the words, but it was impossible. I don't recall ever trying to say 'I love you,' but now that I wanted to, I saw how difficult it was. As I tried to speak the words, it was as if my mind and body were doing everything in their power to make sure those words did not leave my mouth. The harder I tried to say the words, the more my mind and tongue froze. "I don't know why, but it's too hard to say those words. I can't do it," I said, trying to pull away.

Manu squeezed and held me tightly. "Aloha au ia 'oe." Hearing the words "I love you" in Hawaiian seemed easier for me to receive, but I still couldn't reciprocate.

Manu finally released me and Elder Balane gave me an encouraging pat on the back. "Elder Taylor, to love is to make one's heart vulnerable to being hurt," Manu said as he pulled the truck back onto the road. "You must have the courage to love. To avoid the pain of loss and hurt is to also avoid the joy of acceptance and love."

"What about my 'I love you?'" Elder Balane said with a laugh.

Manu chuckled and assured Elder Balane of his love for him. Then he cleared his throat and began the day's lesson.

"There are some, in Western civilization, who view the way of life of ancient Hawai'i as primitive," he said. "Ancient Hawai'i may not be considered a technologically advanced society, but they were, without question, a society that was culturally and spiritually advanced. An advance in technology does not equal an advance in knowledge, happiness, or fulfillment. In fact, in a world of constant change and technological advancement, much ancient wisdom has been lost. What many have defined as progress has actually been deterioration. As you learn the way of Aloha, you will see clearly who is advanced and who is primitive."

I nodded in agreement, thinking of several people I knew who spent most of their time playing video games or watching TV.

"The greatest advancement of our day may occur when we embrace the technology of Aloha. The principles of Aloha connect us in a more powerful way with God, family, and communities than any technology can," Manu said, slowing to turn off the main road. Instinctively, I braced myself for a jolting ride, remembering the last drive Manu had taken us on.

"Technology is ever-changing. Principles are never-changing." Manu continued, his voice clear and steady, despite the changing terrain of the road underneath us. "The template for joyful living is an ancient truth to discover, not a new technique to create. There are many things technology will never replace or duplicate. No technology will ever replace or match the uniting power of a hug. The affirming and welcoming sensations of an embrace warms the heart, lifts the spirit, and heals the body. The hug is the Hawaiian handshake, but it is much more than a greeting. It is an expression of love, trust, hospitality, and family. A hug creates a connection, emotion, and message that a handshake or words cannot duplicate."

Manu noticed Elder Balane and I bracing ourselves against the dash of his truck and smiled. "We're nearly there. While we have only traveled about ten miles, it can take a while on these rough, dirt trails. This will be one of our longest drives."

I held back a groan and exchanged a look with Elder Balane. While the drive was rough, the message Manu was sharing was well worth it.

After about forty minutes of driving, we neared a beach on the east side of the island. I could see the ocean, as well as the island of Maui across the channel. This beach was much different from the large, sandy beach at Polihua. While Polihua was tranquil, with vast fine white sand that sat undisturbed against a restless ocean, the water and terrain in front of us were peppered with large black rocks of various shapes and sizes and a small beach consisting of tiny reddish brown rocks.

We exited the truck and followed Manu as he walked toward the water. "This is the site of an ancient fishing village," he told us, gesturing outward to take in the scene around us. "The ancient Hawaiians were aquafarmers and developed advanced fish husbandry and fish management systems. There are nearly five hundred known fishponds of varying size and preservation throughout the islands. One of these ancient loko i'a (fish ponds) is right before us."

"All I see is a large group of scattered rocks through the water.

Where are the fish ponds?" I asked, raising a hand to shadow my eyes as I squinted into the sun.

Manu shook his head. "The ancient sites and wisdom of Lāna'i are like the Naha Fishpond—not easy to see for the untrained or inexperienced eyes." He smiled as I dropped my hand to my side. "But they are always present for those who have eyes to see. As says the Savior, 'He that hath ears to hear, let him hear.[10] He that hath eyes to see, let him see.'[11] 'For by my Spirit will I enlighten them, and by my power will I make known unto them...those things which eye has not seen, nor ear heard, nor yet entered into the heart of man.'"[12]

Elder Balane moved forward, his eyes still searching for the fishing pond. "I guess I don't have eyes to see," he said with a wry smile.

"Many come to Naha Beach and never see the ancient fish ponds," Manu said, stepping forward and clapping a hand on Balane's back. "Many come to Hawai'i and return home with nothing more than a tan and some souvenirs. They are like those who the prophet Ezekiel said, '[They have] eyes to see, and see not; they have ears to hear, and hear not.'[13] They miss the wisdom of Aloha that is all around them. Do you want to have eyes to see, ears to hear, and hearts to receive?" Manu asked.

Elder Balane and I nodded our heads. Once Manu pointed out the formations and locations of the fish ponds, they could easily be identified for what they were.

"Elder Taylor, have you ever been snorkeling?" Manu asked.

"No, but I'd like to," I answered.

"I would love to take you guys snorkeling, but it's obviously against mission rules," he said. "Hawai'i has some of the best snorkeling and scuba diving in the world. On occasion, while snorkeling, you'll see a large school of fish swimming in unison. It's a miraculous site to watch as the fish quickly shift directions in perfect harmony. It appears as if there is a force at the center of the school, controlling the change in movements. Zion is like a school of fish. In Zion, the people are 'of one heart and one mind'[14] and live in unity and perfect harmony. The force at the center of Zion is Jesus Christ, and they move in unison as they live the principles of Heaven."

Manu settled in on the rocky beach and Elder Balane and I sat down beside him. He stared out at the horizon, his arms resting on his knees. We waited in silence for him to continue, taking in the sounds of the ocean and the distant singing birds.

"The spirit of Aloha is the spirit of Zion," he said. "The ancient Hawaiians lived with lōkāhi, which means 'oneness and loving cooperation.' Elder John H. Groberg illustrates this principle as he describes a lesson he learned as a young missionary traveling on a sailboat in the Tongan islands."

Manu pulled out a well-worn book. "I'd like to read something to you." He flipped to a dog-eared page and cleared his throat. "Elder Groberg wrote, 'We would always pray for protection, success, and good seas and wind to take us to our destination. Once I asked the Lord to bless us with a good tail wind so we could get to Foa quickly. As we got underway, one of the older men said, 'Elder Groberg, you need to modify your prayers a little.'

"'How's that?' I replied.

"'You asked the Lord for a tail wind to take us rapidly to Foa. If you pray for a tail wind to Foa, what about the people who are trying to come from Foa to Pangai? They are good people, and you are praying against them. Just pray for a good wind, not a tail wind.'

"That taught me something important. Sometimes we pray for things that will benefit us but may hurt others. We may pray for a particular type of weather, or to preserve someone's life, when that answer to our prayer may hurt someone else. That's why we must always pray in faith, because we can't have true, God-given faith in something that is not according to His will. If it's according to His will, all parties will benefit. I learned to pray for a good wind and the ability to get there safely, not necessarily a tail wind.'"[15]

Manu set the book down beside him. "The ancient Hawaiians had an attitude of 'what is best for us' not 'what is best for me'—a way of life that produced joy and abundance for all," he explained. "Much of the world operates with a belief in scarcity. Many believe, 'If I win, you lose and if you win, I lose.' However, the Lord has shown us 'a more excellent way,'[16] the way of Aloha, the way of Zion.

"As we learn the principles of lōkāhi and Aloha, we will live in abundance. The ancient fish ponds produced enough fish for everyone on the island," Manu said, pointing toward the ponds before us. "The Savior declares, 'I am come that they might have life, and that they might have it more abundantly.'[17] Abundance is about creation and production, not consumption. We are not to simply produce as much as we need, but we are to produce as much as we can and use the excess to lift our fellowman and build the Kingdom of God. The gospel of Jesus Christ moves us past the focus of only providing for our needs to becoming abundantly productive so that we have surplus to serve others.

"The goal of producing is not to lift ourselves above another but to elevate all. The Lord wants all His children to live in abundance. We should strive to work toward the state found among the followers of Christ in the New Testament where 'all the believers were one in heart and mind. No one claimed that any of his possessions was his own, but they shared everything they had…There were no needy persons among them.'[18]

"These scriptures from the New Testament contain another key element to the way of Aloha. It states, 'No one claimed that any of his possessions was his own.'[19] The ancient Hawaiians recognized that everything was God's. In ancient Hawai'i, it was understood that all land belonged to God. The idea of buying and selling land was not even considered. How can you sell something that is God's? The management and use of the land is a stewardship."

"That's a totally foreign concept in the mainland," I said.

Manu nodded sadly. "This is a principle and cultural tradition we have tried to teach our children. A few months ago, my son was jumping on the furniture and I heard my wife say, 'Stop jumping on my couch.' My five-year-old responded, 'It's not your couch.' My wife, thinking our son was talking back to her, responded, 'What did you say?' My son answered, 'It's not your couch. It's Jesus's couch.' My wife quickly replied, 'Then stop jumping on Jesus's couch.'"

We all laughed at Manu's son's clever innocence and his wife's quick retort.

"I was excited to hear my son's response, because he understood the powerful truth that we own nothing," Manu said, his mouth curling into a proud smile. "It's all the Lord's. President George Q. Cannon, First Counselor in the First Presidency, taught that riches have 'a very corrupting effect upon the human heart, and it requires a very pure people to be as honest, virtuous, humble and upright when surrounded by luxury and wealth... Always remember that your lives, your ability, the food you eat, the water you drink, the clothes you wear, the earth you tread, the air you breathe, are all the Lord's... Then, whether you are rich or poor will make no difference... You will look upon yourselves as stewards, and if you have a hundred dollars in your hands, you will say, this is the Lord's... If you have a million dollars, you will feel the same. And where people have this feeling, riches cannot hurt them. Latter-day Saints must have this kind of faith and feeling, or they cannot build up Zion and be the people the Lord is desirous they should be.'[20]

"The ancient Hawaiians understood that they didn't own the fish ponds or the fish they contained. They were God's. We are often caught up in the 'mine, mine, mine' mentality, allowing greed and selfishness into our hearts. Once we can say, 'It is the Lord's' instead of, 'It is mine,' we're freed from our attachment to earthly possessions, and, instead, we can focus on heavenly treasures.[21] There is no 'mine,' for everything is the Lord's.

"The ancient Hawaiians provide a powerful example of a community and culture that lived in cooperation, harmony, and unity with God and each other. The ancient Hawaiians did not view society as many separate individuals, but as one family. I'm sure you have heard the Hawaiians call people auntie, uncle, and cousin, even though there is no traditional family bloodline. This is because Hawaiians know we are one big ʻohana (family) of God. ʻOhana comes from the highly reverenced word ʻohā. ʻOhā is a word for the ancient taro root from which all taro has sprung. The taro plant was a staple of life to the ancient Hawaiians and was a main source of food and medicine. The word ʻohana signifies that all people come from the same root—God. No matter how many offshoots come from the ʻohā, they all come from the original root. Many of the Hawaiian dictionaries reference the book of Isaiah to explain ʻohā as the branches that grow out of the root of Christ.[22] Christ is the vine and we are the branches.[23] So whether a person is your first cousin or twentieth cousin, he or she is still your brother or sister—your ʻohana. There is a family connection with all people, as we all come from the root and vine of Christ."

"That's a beautiful way of looking at the people around us," Elder Balane said.

"I have a question for you, Elders," Manu said. "If your mom cut you off in traffic, would you honk your horn and yell at her?"

"Of course not," I answered with a laugh. Elder Balane nodded his agreement.

"Now, what if it was a stranger?" Manu asked.

"I guess I might honk my horn?" I answered.

"I probably would, too," Elder Balane admitted.

"In Hawaii, there is no horn honking because there are no strangers. We are all ʻohana. Have you noticed a difference driving in Hawaii?" Manu asked.

"One of the first things I noticed when I arrived in Hawaiʻi was how friendly all the drivers were," I said. "It was a culture shock—in a good way."

"When I first visited Salt Lake City, I experienced a bit of culture shock myself," Manu said, shaking his head. "I was honked at more in a few days than during decades of driving in the islands. Would you agree that no horn honking and more Aloha behind the wheel would make the mainland a better place?"

"Yes," Elder Balane and I said in unison.

"When you view everyone as a member of your 'ohana (family), you act differently. In Ancient Hawai'i, there was a foundational phrase and teaching—*Aloha mai ke akua ipo.* Again, Hawaiian words and phrases have layers of meaning. This phrase would encompass three statements of the Savior. 'Thou shalt love the Lord thy God with all thy heart [and] thou shalt love thy neighbour as thyself,'[24] 'Whatever you wish that others would do to you, do also to them,'[25] and 'Inasmuch as ye have done it unto one of the least of these my brethren, ye have done it unto me.'[26] Now I have another question for you Elders: What is the population of the world?"

"I'm not sure, around five billion?" I answered.

"Not even close. Elder Balane, what is your guess?"

"How about ten billion?" Elder Balane said.

"You're going the wrong direction, Elders. Ponder the phrase 'Aloha mai ke akua ipo' as you ask yourself, 'What is the population of the world?' Think like a Hawaiian, not like a mainland college student," Manu said, smiling.

We both sat in silence, pondering. After a few minutes, Elder Balane blurted out in excitement, "Two! The population of the world is two!"

"Very good. The population of the world is two—Jesus Christ and you. What you do to another, you do to God. If Christ cuts you off in traffic, would you honk your horn at him? If Christ was the victim of a natural disaster, would you help Him? If Christ was in prison, would you visit him? If Christ was hungry, would you feed him?"

We didn't answer Manu. We didn't need to. Instead, we turned our gazes out to the ocean and pondered his questions. I knew this simple principle would change how I viewed and treated others. I was beginning to be filled with a little greater Aloha.

"Well, our time is up for today," Manu said, rising to his feet and dusting off. "It is time to head back for dinner. We can continue our discussion on the long drive back."

We stood as well and made our way to Manu's truck. Once we were all settled and on the road, heading toward Manu's home, he picked up where he'd left off.

"When a society lives with Aloha, there is no need for many rules and laws. The ancient Hawaiians lived by a few simple principles," he said. "I'm sure you're familiar with the statement by Joseph Smith, 'I teach them correct principles, and they govern themselves.'[27] These words of Joseph Smith were recorded by John Taylor. Brigham Young also provided insights into this saying when he wrote, 'The question was asked a great many times of Joseph Smith, by gentlemen who came to see him and his people, 'How is it that you can control your people so easily? It appears that they do nothing but what you say; how is it that you can govern them so easily?' Said he, 'I do not govern them at all. The Lord has revealed certain principles from the heavens by which we are to live in these latter days. The time is drawing near when the Lord is going to gather out His people from the wicked, and He is going to cut short His work in righteousness, and the principles which He has revealed I have taught to the people and they are trying to live according to them, and they control themselves.'[28] Zion is established as the principles of Heaven are taught and lived."

"So will there be police in Zion?" I asked, trying to imagine a world that had no need of them.

"Another term for police is law enforcement. In Zion, there is no need for law enforcement because they live by principles—there are no laws to enforce. In the ancient Hawaiian code of Aloha, there were no 'thou shalt not' statements. If the principles of Heaven are lived, there is no need for a list of dos and don'ts. If you're in a society that needs laws and law enforcement, that society is telestial and terrestrial in nature. One who needs rules and laws is one who needs discipline. One who lives the celestial law of principles would be called a disciple. So, Elders, are you one who needs to be disciplined with rules, or are you a disciple who lives principles?"

"I'm striving to be a disciple, but I know I fall short. As a missionary, we have many rules to follow," I said.

"So, are rules bad?" Elder Balane asked.

"It depends," Manu answered. "Rules are a blessing to the young, the inexperienced, or the spiritually immature. The rules automatically apply higher principles to many of life's common situations. This they do in a predetermined and almost mechanical manner that does not require much judgment or discernment on the part of those who keep them: 'A rule is a rule.' A prime example of righteousness by rules would be the Law of Moses, including the Ten Commandments, which was given to spiritually immature Israel in the wilderness.[29]

"Rules are good when they lead us to principle-based righteousness, but they're evil when they become an end, in and of themselves, as was the case with the Pharisees in the New Testament. The Pharisees were so focused on obedience to the law that they rejected and crucified their law giver. Even though the Pharisees were strictly obedient to rules, they were continually rebuked by the Savior. On one occasion, the Savior declared, 'Except your righteousness shall exceed the righteousness of the scribes and Pharisees, ye shall in no case enter into the kingdom of Heaven.'[30] Obedience to rules is terrestrial righteousness at best and often leads to disobedience and a telestial state.

"For example, when Nephi was directed by the Holy Ghost to slay Laban, he could have easily justified not following the directive because the law clearly states, 'Thou shalt not kill.'[31] If he insisted on being obedient to the law, he would have disobeyed God and thus would have moved to a telestial state of disobedience. Nephi had to violate the law to follow God. Had a Pharisee responded to Nephi's action, he would have declared Nephi a great sinner, worthy of death for breaking the law. But it was by breaking the law that he was obedient. Breaking the law is not an option for a Pharisee. Had Nephi tried to explain to the Pharisees that God told him to kill Laban, they would have declared such remarks as blasphemy, for God would never tell someone to violate the law—a law given by the prophet Moses. A Pharisee would declare that Nephi had obviously listened to the devil."

Manu paused to let this new perspective sink in.

"I'm afraid there are many Pharisees in the Lord's church today who are so focused on obedience to rules that they miss living the principles the rules are trying to teach," he said. "For your righteousness to exceed that of a Pharisee, you must become a disciple who acts and leads, not simply a follower of rules and commands. Today's Pharisees may faithfully attend church every week, fulfill their callings, pay their tithing, and do what they are told, but they may also walk past the man who was robbed and left half dead on the side of the road—as did the priest and Levite in Jesus's parable of the good Samaritan—because they're not the man's home teacher or were not asked to help by the Bishop. We must be disciples who act, not followers who are acted upon. Christ does not want us to simply follow rules and commandments. Christ encourages us to use our agency and creativity to serve and build His kingdoms, saying, 'Men should be anxiously engaged in a good cause, and do many things of their own free will, and bring to pass much righteousness... He that doeth not anything until he is commanded...the same is a slothful and not a wise servant.'[32]

"For example, the Lord has given the law of tithing. Tithing is a rule-based law that is designed to help us live the principle of consecration. The law of tithing could be compared to training wheels on a bicycle. The training wheels are designed for the inexperienced to help them learn to ride. Once the person learns to ride, the training wheels are removed. Training wheels are meant to be temporary. Rules and laws should also be temporary. We should strive to progress past rule-based obedience to principle-based obedience. We commit to live the law of consecration in the temple, but it is up to each of us to take the initiative to create a plan to live this principle."

We pulled off the bumpy dirt road and back onto the main road. I stared out the windshield in front of me, beginning to recognize the scenery. My heart sank as I realized we were almost to Manu's house, which meant a delicious dinner but also the end of the day's lesson.

"There is a small group of Hawaiians that has remained secluded from the rest of the world. They live on the island of Ni'ihau, located eighteen miles southwest of Kaua'i, across the Kaulakahi Channel. It's the smallest inhabited island in Hawai'i. The island is eighteen miles long and ranges from three to six miles wide. Their culture and privacy have been carefully guarded for hundreds of years in an attempt to preserve and perpetuate the Hawaiian way of life. Outsiders can only visit with personal permission from the island's owners, and that is rarely given. This limited access has earned Ni'ihau the title of the forbidden island. Here you can get a glimpse into a society that seeks to live by some of the ancient Hawaiian principles.

"Ni'ihau is the only community left in the world that speaks Hawaiian as their first language. Unlike the rest of Hawaii, English is a foreign language there. Ni'ihau has never been heavily populated due to its dry weather conditions. In 1875, the island had 350 native Hawaiians. Today there are approximately 100 residents who live in a close-knit, God-centered community. The

Niihauans traverse their island on horseback or bicycles. Ni'ihau has no paved roads, no privately-owned vehicles, no stores, no restaurants, no doctors, no fire department, no indoor plumbing, no hotels, and no commercial buildings, but it does have plenty of Aloha. As a result, there are also no police, no jails, and no crime."

"It sounds amazing," Elder Balane said. "I wonder if missionaries will ever have the chance to go there."

Manu turned into his small driveway and parked the truck. Before getting out, he shared one final thought. "Our discussion on principles and rules reminds me of this quote: 'As to methods, there may be a million and then some, but principles are few. The man who grasps principles can successfully select his own methods. The man who tries methods, ignoring principles, is sure to have trouble.'[33] The simple principles of lōkāhi (unity), 'ohana (family), and Aloha mai ke akua ipo (golden rule) when understood and lived, create a place of paradise, a place of peace, a place of love, a place of friendship, and a place of Zion."

Elder Balane and I followed Manu into his house. It was time for dinner, but surprisingly I was not hungry. It was amazing to me that, as I focused on things of the Spirit, my physical appetites were minimized. The words of the Master came to my mind when He answered the apostles, who wondered how he could go for long periods without eating or being hungry, saying, "I have meat to eat that ye know not of... My meat is to do the will of him that sent me, and to finish his work."[34]

CHAPTER 5

HALULU HEIAU

"Divine forgiveness is one of the sweetest fruits of the gospel, removing guilt and pain from our hearts and replacing them with joy and peace of conscience."[35]

- Elder Neil L. Andersen

Soon, it was Monday afternoon again. Like the week before, Elder Balane and I rode our bikes to the school to meet Manu. He greeted us with a warm embrace and a joyful Aloha. Though I stiffened in his arms, I was a little more relaxed this time.

We loaded into his truck and began to drive.

"Before we arrive at our destination, I need to tell you about where we're going and how to conduct yourselves at this sacred location," Manu said, his smiling eyes turning serious. "I'm taking you to the Halulu Heiau, which is an ancient Hawaiian temple. Many heiau can be found throughout the islands. A heiau is not a historic artifact, but is a living spiritual site. It's a temple, a place of worship, a place of offering."

He paused to make sure we were taking in the gravity of his words. Elder Balane and I nodded our understanding.

"This site is wahi pana (sacred), so it is very important to be reverent, humble, and compassionate toward the site as well as to each other while there," Manu continued. "You should treat this temple site with the same reverence and respect you would an LDS temple, for a heiau is a place dedicated and consecrated by a kahuna to be a Holy House of the Lord. Many of the locations of heiau are not disclosed and are kept hidden from visitors to preserve and protect them from those who may not understand the sacred nature of these places and the reverence that should be observed. It is hewa (sinful) to speak or act disrespectfully in a place of wahi pana. Hawaiians follow certain procedures to maintain the respect and reverence that should be observed at a heiau and other sacred sites.

"I'm telling you all of this now because once we arrive, we will remain in silence. We will not speak as we approach and enter the heiau, and we will not speak until we are clear of the sacred location. At the top of the hill, behind the heiau, is a place called Kahekili's leap. After we've completed our visit to the heiau, you will follow me to Kahekili's leap. Once we're clear of the temple ground, we can speak.

"Before you enter the heiau, you must first ask God, the ʻāina (land), and the angels present for permission to enter. As you come to the door of the temple, you will meditate and breathe to prepare yourself to pray."

I was excited to participate in such a sacred ritual although I briefly wondered how a person would know if the authorities present did not grant permission to enter.

"Elders, have you ever been called haole while you have been on the islands?" Manu asked.

"Sure, many times," I said.

"Do you know why they call you this?" Manu asked.

"I don't. I just know that it is a derogatory word used to describe white people," I said. Elder Balane nodded beside me.

Manu continued, "Haole is derived from hā'ole, literally meaning 'no breath.' Haole was a term used with contempt for some of the white missionaries who disregarded Hawaiian practices and thus disrespected their temples and religious practices. The white people came to be known as ha-ole (without breath) because after they said their prayers, they did not breathe three times as was customary in ancient Hawai'i.[36] Before the missionaries came, my people used to sit outside their temples for a long time, meditating and preparing themselves before entering. Then they would creep to the altar to offer their petition, and afterwards would again sit a long time outside, this time to 'breathe life' into their prayers. When the Christians came, they just got up, uttered a few sentences, said 'Amen,' and were done. For that reason, my people called them haoles (without breath), or those who failed to breathe life into their prayers."[37]

Manu's story made me stop and consider. How many times had I paused after a prayer to breathe? Or was I like these other missionaries, who went through the motions and then, without pause, returned to my busy day? It struck me, again, how much I had to learn from Manu and this amazing culture around me.

"You will not want to make the same mistake made by earlier missionaries, so take time to prepare yourselves with meditation and breathing before you enter the temple," Manu said. Elder Balane and I nodded fervently.

"To ask permission to enter, you will offer a silent prayer acknowledging that you are at a temple of God, stating who you are, and why you wish to enter," he continued. "Once permission is granted, you will offer a prayer of thanks for the privilege of entering. If you don't receive permission to enter, please remain outside the heiau or ask why you may not enter and seek to correct this—then ask again for permission to enter."

Elder Balane asked the question that had been on my mind earlier. "How will we know if we've been given permission to enter?"

"It's an internal feeling," Manu said. "The answer is felt with the heart, not heard with physical ears. You will know."

I marveled at the sensitivity to the Spirit that was required to take part in the Hawaiian culture.

Returning to the process of entering the temple, Manu said, "Before you enter, remove your shoes and leave them outside to follow the admonition of the Lord, 'Put off the shoes from off thy feet, for the place whereon thou standest is holy ground.'[38] As you enter the temple, be mindful that it is a place of mana (spiritual power). An attitude of humility, respect, and silence helps to connect, feel, and receive mana. As the Psalm states, 'Be still and know that I am God.'[39] The ancient Hawaiians came to the temple to receive mana and to pray. The mana of the temple will become a part of you, and you will become a part of the temple.

"There are many types of heiau. The Halulu Heiau we are going to visit is a pu'uhonua, which is a place of refuge and forgiveness. Ho'oponopono is an ancient Hawaiian practice of forgiveness and reconciliation practiced by kahuna lapa'au (healing priests). Ho'oponopono was practiced by kahuna lapa'au (healing priests) because hala (sin), guilt caused by hala, and not forgiving ourselves or others can make one sick.

"The process of Hoʻoponopono involves five simple statements: confession, remorse, forgiveness, gratitude, and love. As you are in the temple, you should try the practice of Hoʻoponopono. Since you will be seeking forgiveness and reconciliation with God, the five statements in your prayer may be: I have sinned. I am sorry. Please forgive me. Thank you. I love you.

"The practice of Hoʻoponopono is also used to achieve reconciliation and forgiveness between persons with whom there is a conflict. For reconciliation with your spouse, the five Hoʻoponopono statements may be: I lost my temper. I am sorry. Please forgive me. Thank you. I love you.

"A necessary practice of the Hawaiians when visiting a sacred site is to leave a hoʻokupu (offering), so you should provide one while you're in the temple. The highest and most meaningful offering is mai loko mai, which means it comes from within, such as an oath to preserve and live the principles and values related to the sacred site. A life filled with Aloha is the hoʻokupu (offering) of highest value and has much greater meaning than an offering of food or an item of value. What are the offerings we give in LDS temples? Is it not our oaths and commitments to live the gospel of Jesus Christ? The covenants we make in the temple are our offerings.

"Once you have experienced Hoʻoponopono and hoʻokupu and are ready to leave the temple, you should find a place outside the temple to sit and offer a prayer of gratitude and breathe life into the prayers you have offered."

"What does the temple look like?" I asked.

"Just as our words are a very small part of our communication, so a heiau is much more than what you will see," Manu said. "There are no words to describe this sacred place. A heiau is not a place to see—it is a place to experience. To truly understand this sacred place, you must feel its spirit and mana." Manu paused as he turned the truck down an unmarked road. "We're only a few miles from the temple, so let's begin our silence and preparation."

Manu continued driving down the rough, dirt road and eventually pulled off to the side. As I exited the truck, I could see the beauty of the ocean in the distance and feel the serenity of the peaceful landscape. There was no one in sight and no evidence of anyone having traversed this area of the island for quite some time. The trail we followed Manu down was completely overgrown. After several minutes of walking, I could see the temple. Although the roof was no longer in place, I was amazed to see that most of the temple remained intact, its ancient walls formed of intricately placed rocks stacked to perfection. Peace permeated this impressive structure, which overlooked the heavenly view of Lāna'i's south shore.

I reverently advanced toward the temple. The only sounds were our soft breathing and our feet stepping lightly along the dirt path. I found a spot to pray, breathe, and ponder, in preparation to enter this sacred edifice. As I approached the door to request permission to enter, I took several deep breaths and offered this silent prayer: "I am grateful for the privilege to stand at the door of the temple. I am a weak servant of the Lord Jesus Christ. I seek to enter the temple to ask forgiveness of my sins. May I enter the house of the Lord?" As I said the words, "May I enter," warmth and peace permeated my body. I knew I had permission to enter and it struck me how much communication can happen without words.

I removed the shoes from my feet, placed them next to those of Manu and Elder Balane, and walked into the temple. The heiau was filled with a calm, peaceful spirit, like the celestial room of a modern-day temple.

I closed my eyes, cleared my mind, and took in several deep breaths. As I began meditating in preparation to practice Ho'oponopono, the thought entered my mind that I should speak directly to Jesus. I offered these silent words: "Master, I am a sinner, but I don't wish to sin. Please forgive me."

Warmth and love coursed through me, and I heard the words of the Savior as if they were spoken directly to my spirit, saying, "Be of good cheer, your sins are forgiven."[40]

I sat in silence and wonder, tears pouring down my cheeks. I repeated these words in my mind: "Thank you! Thank you! I love you." As I thought these words, I was filled with the love of the Savior—a perfect love and feeling which no words can describe. As I basked in the love and presence of the Savior, the word ho'okupu came into my mind. It was time to give my temple offering. "Master, I am grateful for your compassionate mercy, unconditional love, abounding grace, and perfect forgiveness. Please help me to be as quick to forgive others as you are to forgive me."

After several minutes of quiet contemplation, it was time to exit the temple. As we exited, we picked up our shoes and each found a spot to sit and ponder in silence. Eventually, I felt a hand on my shoulder and looked up to see Manu. It was time to leave.

We walked up a hill and approached the edge of the cliff. "This is Kahekili's leap," Manu said.

I walked slowly to the edge and took a deep breath. Holding tightly onto one of the large rocks, I peered over to the turbulent ocean below. "How far down is it?" I asked.

"It's about sixty-five feet to the water," Manu answered. "This is a place where warriors would prove their bravery by leaping from the cliff into the ocean. As you can see, it's a sheer cliff, but there are rocks at the bottom that extend about fifteen feet out into the ocean. It's necessary to get a running start to clear the rocks below. The fact that the water is shallow (about fifteen feet deep) with sharp rocks on the ocean floor adds to the danger of the jump. This is a significant spot in Lāna'i's history. It recently received much attention as it was the location for the world cliff diving championship."

Elder Balane and I stared down the edge of the cliff. I couldn't see his expression but I felt sure he was thinking the same thing I was: could I make the leap if I needed to?

"Well, that's enough about Kahekili's leap," Manu said, stepping away from the cliff edge. "What was your experience at the temple?"

I was the first to answer. "It's definitely a sacred place of power, healing, and forgiveness."

"You could feel power there," Elder Balane agreed. "I'm glad you explained its sacred nature before we arrived."

Manu nodded. "As I mentioned before, the practice of Ho'oponopono was administered by the kahuna lapa'au (healing priest). There was a kahuna lapa'au at the temple today. Did you recognize His presence?"

"As I pondered in the temple," I said, "I had the impression to speak directly to Jesus. I clearly felt His presence there."

"Yes, indeed," Manu replied. "This promise of Christ was witnessed today: 'For where two or three are gathered together in my name, there am I in the midst of them.'[41] Jesus Christ is the Master Kahuna Lapa'au and He is the source of all healing and forgiveness. The New Testament provides us with many accounts of His divine healing throughout His earthly ministry. Matthew records a man sick of the palsy being brought to Jesus to be healed, 'and Jesus seeing their faith said unto the sick of palsy: Son, be of good cheer, thy sins be forgiven thee...then saith He to the sick of the palsy, Arise, take up thy bed, and go unto thine house.'[42] When people came to Christ for healing, He often first forgave their sins. They asked to be healed physically, but first He healed them spiritually. Christ's greatest gift of healing is forgiveness. Receiving Christ's gift of forgiveness is essential to your physical well-being and the healing of your body."

Manu walked a short distance to a rock that was about the size of a truck. He gestured to it. "Elder Balane, will you please pick up this rock?"

Elder Balane attempted the task with no success. We couldn't help laughing at his fruitless efforts.

"There is a Hawaiian legend that a bearded white man came to earth and carried a large rock weighing several tons from the valley to the top of the mountain," Manu said, resting his hand on the rock. "He was a God among men. The legend continues that those who connect with this God can also carry the rock up the mountain, but that the rock cannot be lifted by physical strength—only by their hearts. I find this legend to be a powerful metaphor for the atonement of Jesus Christ. Christ has taken upon himself the burden of sin. Christ has carried the large rock of sin to the top of the mountain. The penalty for sin has been paid by a God who came among men. You can try all you want to move the huge rock up the mountain with physical force, but you will have no success. It's impossible for the rock of sin to be lifted by physical force or by your works. The rock of sin is lifted by giving your heart to the Lord Jesus Christ and receiving His grace. We don't need to try to bear the weight of sin, for Christ has already borne the weight for us. Those who are seeking to carry the boulder of sin up the mountain need to give heed to the words of the Master, 'Come unto me, all ye that labor and are heavy laden, and I will give you rest. Take my yoke upon you, and learn of me...and ye shall find rest unto your souls. For my yoke is easy, and my burden is light.'[43]

"I see some who insist on carrying the rock up the mountain themselves. These people remind me of those who didn't receive the gift of healing promised by Moses." Manu gave the rock a gentle pat, the sadness of this truth reflected on his face. "The book of Numbers reads, 'And the Lord sent fiery serpents among the people, and they bit the people; and much people of Israel died. Therefore, the people came to Moses, and said, We have sinned, for we have spoken against the Lord, and against thee; pray unto the Lord, that He take away the serpents from us. And Moses prayed for the people. And the Lord said unto Moses, make thee a fiery serpent, and set it upon a pole: and it shall come to pass, that every one that is bitten, when he looketh upon it, shall live. And Moses made a serpent of brass, and put it upon a pole, and it came to pass, that if a serpent had bitten any man, when he beheld the serpent of brass, he lived.'[44] The *Book of Mormon* gives further insight into the incident saying, 'The Lord... prepared a way that they might be healed; and the labor which they had to perform was to look; and because of the simpleness of the way, or the easiness of it, there were many who perished...Now the reason they would not look is because they did not believe that it would heal them.'[45]

"This story is an obvious type of Christ. All they had to do was look to the brass serpent on the cross and they would be healed of their deadly snake bites. Christ has promised that He will heal you of the deadly bite of sin if you will but look to Him with a broken heart and a contrite spirit. He says, 'Though your sins be as scarlet, they shall be as white as snow; though they be red like crimson, they shall be as wool... I will forgive...and I will remember [your] sin no more.'[46] Moroni 6:8 tells us that 'As oft as they repented and sought forgiveness, with real intent, they were forgiven.' In the *Doctrine and Covenants* the Lord declares, 'He who has repented of his sins, the same is forgiven, and I, the Lord, remember them no more.'[47] The book of 1 John reads, 'If we say that we have no sin, we deceive ourselves, and the truth is not in us. If we confess our sins, [Christ] is faithful and just to forgive us our sins...and the blood of Jesus Christ...cleanseth us from all sin.'[48] As we repent and ask the Lord for forgiveness, we will hear the glorious words of the Savior, 'Be of good cheer; thy sins be forgiven thee.'[49]

"If you ever find yourself trying to carry the rock of sin, remember

Christ's grace and receive His healing power of forgiveness. Put down the rock of guilt and pain and offer a prayer of gratitude and praise. Through Christ's grace, you are forgiven. The Lord declares, 'For behold, I, God, have suffered these things for all, that they might not suffer if they would repent...Which suffering caused myself, even God, the greatest of all, to tremble because of pain, and to bleed at every pore, and to suffer both body and spirit.'[50] Christ has paid the price for your sins so you don't have to. The atonement is complete. All who look to the cross of Christ will be healed."

Elder Balane asked Manu, "Why do you think so many people struggle with the idea of grace?"

"One of the difficulties some have with grace is that it's not fair," Manu said. "We often have a hard time accepting Christ's forgiveness and grace because we don't deserve it. But that is the whole point of grace. Christ is giving us something we don't deserve. If we deserved it, it would not be grace. Some want to earn grace by attempting to carry the rock up the mountain, but grace can't be earned. Grace is a gift that is received. Attempting to lift the rock of sin ourselves will not lead to forgiveness and strength, but to sorrow and despair, for we have no power to forgive sins. All you can do to lift the rock of sin is give your heart to the Lord Jesus Christ. Christ has already paid the price of all your sins: past, present, and future. His forgiveness does not need to be earned. It needs to be received."

I nodded. "It's so hard because it's so simple."

Manu smiled. "Well, our time is up for today," he said. "We'd better head home."

I tried to hide my disappointment, but I wanted to continue.

I was on such a spiritual high from the whole experience, I felt like I was floating instead of walking as we followed Manu to his truck.

As we traveled back down the bumpy road, Manu said, "Hawaiʻi is the most secluded land on the planet. California is the closest land mass at 2,390 miles away. Japan is the closest land to the west and is 3,859 miles away. Hawaiʻi remained isolated from the world for centuries until the late 1700s when the islands were discovered by Captain Cook. The ancient Hawaiians were led here by the Lord and are among those spoken of in the *Book of Mormon*: 'The more part of all the tribes [of Israel] have been led away; and they are scattered to and fro upon the isles of the sea; and whither they are none of us knoweth, save that we know that they have been led away.'[51]

"There are many striking similarities between the ancient teachings of Hawaiʻi and those of ancient North American Indians and ancient Israel. Several years ago, after teaching a conference on ancient Hawaiʻi in the mainland to a group of Native American Indians, one of the chiefs said to me, 'What you have taught us is what our elders speak of as the old ways.'[52]

"Lānaʻi is sometimes referred to as the forgotten island, but it is experiences, like today, that remind me the Lord has not forgotten this beautiful island. Jesus declares, 'Yea, they may forget, yet will I not forget thee, O house of Israel. Behold, I have graven thee upon the palms of my hands.'"[53]

CHAPTER 6

GARDEN OF THE GODS

"Whatever you ask the Father in My name He will give you. Until now you have asked nothing in My name. Ask, and you will receive, that your joy may be full."[54]

- Jesus Christ

We had a busy week of teaching, tracting, serving, and preparing two investigators for baptism. Elder Balane and I eagerly anticipated another adventure with Manu, but we first needed to buy groceries and visit the laundromat. Our laundry took longer than expected, so we rode our bikes directly to the school to meet Manu, carrying our laundry bags in one hand and steering our bikes with the other. We were a few minutes late. Manu was waiting for us in the parking lot.

"Looks like you brought me a present," Manu said as we pulled up.

"Sure. If you want some white shirts and slacks that you could have worn when you were eight," I said with a smile.

Manu laughed as we tossed our laundry bags into the back of his truck. "We'll be traveling on rough terrain again today, so you'd better keep your laundry with you in the cab."

We grabbed our laundry back out and climbed into the truck. We spent an awkward moment trying to shove the laundry into the space at our feet and buckle in. Manu waited patiently until we were settled.

It only took a minute for the paved road of Lāna'i City to end and the dirt road to begin. The road became more rugged each minute we drove, with sizeable potholes and ruts canvassing the surface.

As we ascended, we bounced, bumped, and rocked, passing what seemed to be endless miles of shrubs, grass, and red dirt. Without warning, the vegetation was gone, replaced with hundreds of beautiful rock formations, boulders, and spires. This assortment of diverse rock formations was scattered across the top of the mountain as if they had rained down from Heaven. The striking hues of the landscape radiated a deep red, with hints of orange and purple. These colors were accentuated by the contrasting greens and blues in the surrounding valley, sky, and ocean.

Manu parked. Once we were gathered outside the truck, he gestured to the scene before us. "Welcome to Keahiakawelo, the Garden of the Gods," he said.

This landscape was different from anything I'd ever seen. It was as if we'd traveled to a different planet. The garden's beauty went beyond merely its external appeal. The Garden of the Gods had a distinctive spirit of peace and serenity. There was a feeling that the heavens and the earth connected here in some way.

Manu motioned for us to follow him, and we came to a rock formation, which seemed to rest on the pinnacle of the topography. The vista was breathtaking. It was a clear day and Moloka'i could be seen easily across the ocean channel. Manu pointed into the distance. As we gazed outward, we could see the island of O'ahu.

After taking in this panoramic feast, Manu had us surround the rock formation, facing inward.

"One of the legends told of Keahiakawelo is that God placed each of the rocks here for a divine purpose," he said. "It's also believed that the formation we are gathered around was a prayer altar for one of Lāna'i's ancient kahunas. You obviously know that we pray surrounding altars in the LDS temples. The ancient Hawaiians also prayed around altars, and families had altars for prayer called Pule Kuahu. Under the Law of Moses, the altar was used for offering animal sacrifice. Today, with the Law of Moses fulfilled, we no longer offer animal sacrifices. Have you ever wondered why we still pray around an altar?"

"Today we pray around an altar to make the offering of a broken heart and a contrite spirit," I said.

Manu nodded. "When we were at the heiau (temple), we talked about the importance of ho'okupu (offerings). Our offering is submitting our will to the will of the Father. 'Prayer is the act by which the will of the Father and the will of the child are brought into correspondence with each other. The object of prayer is not to change the will of God'[55] but to know the will of God. As we're gathered around this altar, I'll share with you a dream I had that helped me better understand prayer."

Manu paused, his gaze growing distant as he recalled the dream. Elder Balane and I looked on in hushed silence, eager to hear what he wanted to share with us.

"My dream began as I stood at what is often referred to as the pearly gates of Heaven," Manu said. "As I stood at the closed gate, I saw a man in vivid white clothing, approaching from the other side. As he got closer, I was overwhelmed by the power and beauty of his countenance and fell to my knees. When the man spoke, his words not only penetrated my ears, but my entire being. Speaking to me both physically and spiritually, he said, 'Manu, arise to thy feet. There is only one before whom you should kneel, and that is the Master, Jesus Christ. I am His servant, Peter.'

"As I rose to my feet, the gate swung open. Peter greeted me with an embrace and said, 'Welcome home, my brother.'

"I returned the embrace and was filled with the pure love of Christ that exceeded any possible earthly description. As our embrace concluded, I asked, 'Where am I?'

"Peter answered with a smile, 'This is Heaven.'

"'So, am I dead?'

"'No, you are not dead. You are dreaming. I have been instructed to show you one building in Heaven. Would you like to see it?'

"As Peter asked the question, I was consumed by the Spirit and quickly answered in the affirmative. Peter instructed me to follow him. I walked at his right side and we passed through the pearly gates, following a path of gold. Looking ahead, I could see that the gold path led to a large building up on a hill. The path was lined with flowers, grass, shrubs, and trees that were unlike anything I'd encountered on earth. These plants were not only vibrant and bright, but they radiated color, light, and spirit. There are millions of colors that await us in Heaven not found on the earth.

"Gentle music filled the air. I couldn't discern a source for the music, but it filled the immensity of space around us. The sound was not directional. It was as if I was underwater in a swimming pool, but instead of being surrounded by water, I was submerged in music.

"Unlike earthly melodies, these sounds were received more by my spirit than by my ears, radiating to all my senses. 'I can't tell you how different it is from what you hear on earth! It feels like joy, looks like love, smells like flowers, and dances like butterflies. Music there is alive! You can even taste it.'[56]

"We approached a building and I was astonished by its immense size, brilliant architecture, and splendid beauty. I was surprised to see my name, Manu Nāpela, written on the front of it.

"I asked Peter, 'Why is my name on this building?'

"'This is your heavenly warehouse, Manu. There is one of these warehouses for each person on earth, and each warehouse is identified with that person's name.'

"'What you call a warehouse looks to me more like a palace,' I exclaimed. 'It exceeds in every way any building I have seen on earth.'

"Peter nodded. 'What you say is true, but wait until you see the palaces of Heaven. They are much more splendid than this warehouse.'

"The gold path ended in front of two large double doors. The doors were set inside a beautiful arch. The hinges, symbols, and door knobs had the brilliance of gold. The doors reminded me of the exterior doors of the Salt Lake temple. However, they were a color I'd never seen. Pointing to the door, I asked, 'Peter, what is the name of this color?'

"Peter answered, 'Ahina. Isn't it beautiful?'

"The word sounded Hawaiian although I didn't recognize it. Discerning my thoughts, Peter explained, 'The ancient Hawaiian language was derived from the language of Heaven and thus, the similarities. Ahina is the name we use for this color in Heaven.'

"I noticed writing on the door knobs in a language I couldn't read. 'What is written on the doorknobs?' I asked.

"Turning the knob, Peter answered, 'It says 'Holiness to the Lord' written in the language of Heaven.'

"Peter opened the door, held it open, and motioned for me to enter.

"As I entered, I was engulfed by crisp, fresh air that invigorated my body and spirit. I turned my head from side to side in awe and wonder. The building was filled with thousands upon thousands of shelves. The shelves were in perfectly uniform rows with exact spacing and symmetry. All angles appeared to form a perfect square. I looked down one of the rows; the shelf continued as far as my eyes could see and appeared to have no end. Each of the shelves was filled with beautifully wrapped gifts of all shapes, colors, and sizes.

"Peter followed me into the warehouse and closed the door behind him. I turned and asked, 'May I look at one of the gifts?'

"Peter answered, 'Of course. That is why we are here.'

"I walked to one of the gifts that caught my attention. The wrapping paper, ribbons, and decorations formed exquisite color combinations. In this one small gift, there were more colors than all the colors visible on earth. I noticed an ornate tag attached to the gift. On the tag was my name in elegant, hand-written cursive. I looked at the tags on the surrounding presents and found that each of the tags had my name on them as well. I turned to Peter and asked, 'What are all these gifts with my name on them?'

"Peter brought me a chair that was sitting along one of the walls and asked me to be seated. Once I'd taken my seat, Peter answered, 'These are all the gifts and blessings from God that you failed to receive.'

"As I heard his words, my heart sank. A wave of pain flashed through my body at the thought of having rejected gifts from my God and my Savior. I looked into Peter's eyes. With great concern, I said, 'I would never knowingly reject a gift from God. Why didn't I receive these gifts?'

"Peter came to my side, placed his hand upon my shoulder, and said, 'I know, Manu. You have a pure heart and real intent. Please let me teach you how the warehouse works. Follow me.'

"I followed Peter as he walked down and across several aisles. Although he walked at a quick pace, he didn't seem in a hurry. When he finally stopped, I noticed that all the shelves in this particular area were empty.

"'Why are these shelves empty?' I asked.

"'These shelves contained all the blessings and gifts God gave to you which required no effort or work on your part. Thus, the shelves are empty because they were all given to you while you were on earth,' answered Peter.

"I frowned, trying to understand. 'Well, what about all the other shelves full of gifts? Why wasn't I given them?'

"'Some of the gifts required work or effort on your part before they could be obtained,' Peter answered.

"We walked to a new section of the warehouse and Peter had me look at the tags on the gifts. I saw my name on one of the tags and on another tag, was written the requirement to receive the gift. The first tag I read said, 'Pray and ask for it.' I looked at each tag to find the same statement: 'Pray and ask for it.'

"'You mean all I had to do to receive all the gifts in this warehouse was to pray and ask for them?' I said.

"'You're getting ahead of me,' Peter replied. 'This section of the warehouse contains all the gifts God wanted to give you; and all that was required to receive them was to pray and ask for them. Heaven has warehouses full of undelivered gifts because many have not learned that God has countless gifts to give if one will only ask. My fellow apostle, James taught, '...ye have not, because ye ask not.'[57]'

"'Peter, how was I supposed to ask for these gifts when I didn't even know they existed?' I asked incredulously.

"'You must pray and ask to know what to pray for,' Peter said. 'You need to pray to find out what is in your warehouse. You should pray and ask God to tell you what gifts to pray for. It is a wise man who knows what to pray for, and you can know what to pray for by the Spirit.[58]'

"'There is something I still don't understand. My warehouse is full of gifts, yet there were times on earth when I prayed and asked for things and did not receive them. Can you please explain this?' I asked.

"'It could have been one of two reasons,' Peter said. 'Either you were asking for something that was not in your warehouse,[59] or what you were asking for required more than simply asking to receive.'

"To demonstrate his point, Peter took me to another section of the warehouse and said, 'As I mentioned earlier, God has placed a requirement for the receipt of each gift. When you receive any gift from God, it's a result of fulfilling this requirement. Asking in prayer is only one of many possible requirements.'

"I began to look at the tags on the gifts in this section and found the requirements: get married, attend church, start a business, care for the poor, adopt a child, and visit a widow. Some of the gifts contained a long series of requirements to obtain the gift.

"As I looked through the many tags, Peter stood off to one side and related an experience from his earthly ministry: 'One day, a man brought his son who was possessed by a devil to me and the other disciples, and asked us to cure him. But we were unable to. Then Jesus came and rebuked the devil and the child was cured that very hour. We asked Jesus, 'Why were we unable to cast out the devil and cure the child?' Jesus replied, 'Howbeit this kind goeth not out but by prayer and fasting.'[60] From this experience, I learned that gifts can require more than asking to receive.'

"Peter paused to let his words sink in. I stopped looking through the tags on the gifts and turned my full attention to Peter. 'Another example can be found in the translation of the *Book of Mormon*,' he said. 'Soon after [Oliver] Cowdery began work on the *Book of Mormon*, he wanted to exercise the...gift of translation. Characteristically, Joseph made no effort to monopolize the work...he held out the expectation throughout his life that his followers could receive revelations or see the face of God as he did. The first revelation to Cowdery promised a 'gift if you desire of me, to translate even as my servant Joseph.' Hearing this, Joseph remembered, Cowdery 'became exceedingly anxious to have the power to translate bestowed upon him.' Cowdery tried the experiment but failed. He began and then stopped, apparently mistakenly believing that he needed only to ask God and look in the stone.'[61] Christ explained in a revelation what Oliver's mistake had been. 'Behold, you have not understood; you have supposed that I would give it unto you, when you took no thought save it was to ask me. But, behold, I say unto you, that you must study it out in your mind; then you must ask me if it be right, and if it is right, I will cause that your bosom shall burn within you; therefore, you shall feel that it is right. But if it be not right, you shall have no such feelings, but you shall have a stupor of thought that shall cause you to forget the thing which is wrong; therefore, you cannot write that which is sacred save it be given you from me. Now, if you had known this you could have translated; nevertheless, it is not expedient that you should translate now.'[62]

"My chest burned with fire as the truth of his words engulfed me. 'Oliver was not present to watch Joseph develop and learn to use the gift of translation,' Peter said, shaking his head. 'Oliver arrived after the first one hundred and sixteen pages had been translated by Joseph, and lost by Martin Harris. 'All knowledge and skill are obtained by consistent and determined study and practice, and so the Prophet found it to be the case in the translating of the *Book of Mormon*.'[63] Joseph had to learn how to translate the curious characters on the gold plates.[64] When he first received the plates, he was unsure how to begin. It took time and various attempts to develop a method. Joseph was diligent in his effort but it took much study and practice to learn how to use the gift of translation.[65] Likewise, there are gifts the Lord has for you that require diligent effort to be received.

"'Manu,' Peter said, 'prayer is a form of work, and is an appointed means for obtaining the greatest of God's gifts. Prayer is not to tell God which blessings and gifts He should give you, but to ask for gifts that God is already willing to give and is simply waiting for you to ask for.'[66] One of the most repeated phrases by the Savior is, 'ask and ye shall receive.' This passage is found over forty times in the scriptures.

"'Heaven has a warehouse of gifts for each person on the earth, but sadly many of the gifts are never opened. Some are like the woman who approached Jesus while He was sitting by a well. She didn't recognize Jesus or the gift He had for her. Jesus said to this woman, 'If you only knew the gift God has for you and who you are speaking to, you would ask me, and I would give you.'[67]

"'Manu, I will give you these departing words: You have seen and know the gifts God has for you. As a child of God, accepting His gifts should be natural and instinctive. With the excitement of a child on Christmas morning, you can joyfully open your beautifully wrapped gifts from Heaven. Ask, and it shall be given you; seek, and ye shall find; knock, and it shall be opened unto you.'[68]

"As Peter said these final words, I awoke from my dream and quickly recorded it. It's an experience I will never forget."

Elder Balane and I didn't try to fill the silence that followed. Manu had painted such a beautiful picture of Heaven with his words that I didn't want to come back to reality. Glancing at Elder Balane's tear-filled eyes, I could tell he felt the same.

"What are your thoughts?" Manu asked after several minutes.

"I'm excited to see the many colors and the beauty of Heaven; and I wonder what gifts are in my warehouse," I said in a solemn voice.

"I agree," Elder Balane said. "The question that comes to my mind is, why don't we ask? We're continually told 'ask and ye shall receive,' but I know I'm hesitant to ask."

"I have spent many hours studying and pondering on the command 'ask and ye shall receive,'" Manu said. He moved to sit down on a smaller rock positioned in front of the large one we'd been facing. Elder Balane and I settled in beside him. "I think one of the reasons we don't ask is the belief that we're not worthy or deserving of the gift. A few years ago, a friend of mine said to me, 'I love your yard. It's beautiful.' I told him, 'Not really. There are so many weeds and so much trimming that needs to be done.' He said again, 'No really, I like your yard.' At this point, I realized I had rejected his compliment, and he was trying to give the compliment again to see if I would accept it on the second attempt. I accepted the compliment with a simple 'Thank you.' As I analyzed why I rejected the compliment the first time, I realized I didn't think the yard was worthy or deserving of the compliment. I came up with reasons why the yard was undeserving. Often, we don't ask or don't accept gifts for the same reason. However, if we received a gift because we deserved it, it would no longer be a gift. It would be a wage. Gifts are a form of grace, which means they are something we haven't earned.

"Another reason I've found that some are hesitant to ask is the belief that to ask for more would be selfish or ungrateful. The parable of the cup helped me overcome this false idea. The Lord has many blessings He wants to pour upon us, but we must be willing and able to receive them. For example, let's say God has a gallon of gifts He wants to pour upon you, and the cup you have to receive these gifts in is big enough to hold 1/10 of a gallon. Your cup will be filled to capacity, but will not be able to hold the other 9/10 of the gifts. As you increase the capacity of your cup, the Lord will continue to fill it. Your cup will always be full to the amount you are able and willing to receive. Some with 1/10 of a gallon cup may mistakenly think, 'My cup is full. I don't need to receive anymore.' However, if this ever becomes your attitude, your cup will shrink, the capacity will decrease, and some of the gifts and blessings you previously had will slip over the top of the cup and be lost. We need to continually work to increase the size of our cup so we can receive more and more of the blessings and gifts the Lord wants to pour upon us.

"The Lord teaches this principle in the *Doctrine and Covenants*. He declares that those who receive the celestial, terrestrial, and telestial glory will all be given a fullness.[69] All our cups will be full, but some will have a telestial cup, some will have a larger terrestrial cup, and others even a larger celestial cup. Each will have a fullness, but to those who do not receive as much as they could have, the Lord declares, 'They shall...enjoy that which they are willing to receive, because they were not willing to enjoy that which they might have received. For what doth it profit a man if a gift is bestowed upon him, and he receive not the gift? Behold, he rejoices not in that which is given unto him, neither rejoices in him who is the giver of the gift.'[70]

"The Lord pours the same blessings of celestial glory onto

each person, but the blessings each person receives will be different depending on the amount they are willing and able to receive. Once their cup reaches capacity, the rest will spill over the top of the cup. Thus, the gift is bestowed upon them, but they receive not the gift. The twenty-third Psalm says, '…my cup runneth over.'[71] This provides an image of what happens when the gifts poured upon us by the Lord are greater than our capacity to receive.

"So, is it selfish to enlarge your cup to receive the blessings God wants to give you? No. It's rejecting God's gifts that is selfish. Is the person who receives celestial glory ungrateful? Telestial glory is amazing and surpasses anything we can imagine. Shouldn't we be satisfied to receive the telestial glory? Of course not. It is not ungrateful to want to receive all that God wants to give us. Imagine what would occur if someone handed you a beautifully wrapped present and you handed it back and said, 'I don't want it.' When you reject or fail to receive a gift, you hurt not only yourself but also the giver of the gift. When you are a good and grateful receiver, you deepen your relationship with Jesus Christ."

"Manu, this reminds me of a story my first companion, Elder Kirchhausen, told me when I first arrived in Laie," I said. "He told me, 'You need to be prepared to eat a lot. You can't even comprehend how much you'll eat. You need to be able to eat several large Thanksgiving meals every night. They prepare a feast when the missionaries come to their home. The Hawaiians know they're blessed for feeding a servant of the Lord Jesus Christ. They want you to eat a lot because they believe the more you eat, the more blessings they'll receive. You won't be able to eat like you need to at first, but your stomach will stretch and grow. Over time, you'll be able to eat more.' He then told me about a small Japanese elder who served in Laie and was not liked by the members because he didn't eat very much. Elder Miyagi wanted to be able to eat more, so he would come home and do different things to expand his stomach."

"This could be the parable of the stomach," Manu said, laughing. "Just as an elder must stretch his stomach to receive all the food the Hawaiian people want to give him, so you must stretch and grow to receive all the gifts Christ has to give you. Just as the Hawaiian people are sad if you're not able to eat all the food they have prepared, so is Christ sad if you're unable to receive the gifts He has prepared for you. To receive the vast reservoir of gifts the Lord has, you must expand and grow. The Hawaiian people are disappointed if you say, 'I am full.' Likewise, the Lord is disappointed when we say, 'I am full.' We should continually be expanding our cup for the Lord to pour more into it.

"The Lord teaches this principle in the parable of the talents. In this parable, a lord gave to one of his servants five talents, to another two talents, and to another one talent.[72] The servant who received two talents and the servant who received five talents both received more talents; however, the servant who received one talent hid the talent and received no more. When the day of reckoning arrived, the servant given two talents and the servant given five talents both reported increasing the number of talents they had received, to which the lord said, 'Well done, thou good and faithful servant: thou hast been faithful over a few things, I will make thee ruler over many things: enter thou into the joy of thy lord.'[73] The servant who had hidden his talent, and as a result received no more, earned the rebuke, 'Thou wicked and slothful servant.'[74] The lord then took the talent from him and gave it to the man who had increased his five talents to ten talents and declared, 'For unto every one that hath shall be given, and he shall have abundance: but from him that hath not shall be taken away even that which he hath.'[75] We are constantly either growing or shrinking."

"There are so many people in the world with so little. Isn't it greedy or selfish to want to receive more?" Elder Balane asked.

"I think this thought comes from a belief in scarcity," Manu said. "With a scarcity mindset, you believe that if one person receives more, others have to receive less. This is not true. God is a God of abundance, and He has a reservoir of blessings to give each of His children. God giving more to one of His children in no way limits the gifts He has to give to others."

"So can I ask for a Ferrari and a yacht?" Elder Balane asked with a smile.

Manu chuckled as he shook his head. "The Lord abundantly blesses those who follow Him and the principles of His gospel. However, I don't believe there's a Ferrari or yacht in your warehouse. The world teaches that money is for luxury and leisure, but the Lord teaches that money is for mission and ministry—for service and sacrifice—for gratitude and giving. I don't believe God sent anyone to earth to sit on a yacht. We should be driven by our mission, not by our money. In the *Book of Mormon*, Jacob declared, 'Before ye seek for riches, seek ye for the kingdom of God. And after ye have obtained a hope in Christ ye shall obtain riches, if ye seek them; and ye will seek them for the intent to do good—to clothe the naked, and to feed the hungry, and to liberate the captive, and administer relief to the sick and the afflicted.'[76]

"Here is another analogy that might help." Manu adjusted his position on the rock. "A servant is given a task by his master. The servant completes the task with excellence and returns to his master and says, 'The task is complete. What else can I do for you?' The master is pleased and the servant is given more. The servant completes these tasks and returns to his master and says, 'The tasks are complete, as well as these additional tasks that I saw needed to be done.' The master answers, 'Thank you, my wise and faithful servant.'

"So, is it selfish to ask for more to build the kingdom of God? Of course not. It's being a good, faithful, and diligent servant, and one who will greatly please God!"

"What about the scripture that says it's better to give than to receive?" I asked, squinting up at Manu. The sun had begun to set, the golden rays fading into shades of pink and purple.

"Elder Taylor, the scripture actually reads, 'It is more blessed to give than to receive.'[77] The reason we want to receive is so we can give, and when we give we're blessed. Another translation of this verse says, 'More blessings come from giving than from receiving.'[78]

"I think giving and receiving are equals," he continued. "For every giver, there must be an equal receiver, and, in order to give, we must first receive. In Jesus's parable of the Good Samaritan, the Samaritan helps a man who was robbed of his money and clothes and left half-dead. The Samaritan bound his wounds, cared for him, and took him to an inn. The Samaritan also paid the host two pence, which was two days' wages, to take care of the injured man, and agreed to repay the host if the cost was higher.[79] The Samaritan had to first receive the financial means before he could care for the robbed and injured man. To be good givers, we must be good receivers.

"Well, I hope this answers your questions. I would like to stay and talk further, but our time is up for today," Manu said. Elder Balane and I rose to our feet and I dusted off the seat of my pants.

"Would it be alright if we walk around the garden to take a few pictures?" I inquired.

"That would be fine, but remember, this is a sacred place."

I nodded my understanding. Then we walked around the garden and took pictures of the beautiful rock formations and breathtaking views. The scene was so vast, it wasn't possible to capture in a picture. After Manu took a few pictures of Elder Balane and me as we stood by the rock altar, we headed to Manu's truck to return to Lāna'i City.

We drove in silence for most of the drive back. As Manu turned into his neighborhood, he spoke, "I have a story from the life of Joseph Smith I think you'll enjoy. This story was told by Joseph's first cousin, John Lyman Smith. He often ate at the prophet's home and related this dinner prayer by the prophet during one of his visits, saying, 'I was at play in the room with his son, Joseph, when he called us to him, and we stood, one on each side of him. After he had looked over the table he said, 'Lord, we thank Thee for this Johnny cake, and ask Thee to send us something better. Amen.' The cornbread was cut and I received a piece from his hand. Before the bread was all eaten, a man came to the door and asked if the Prophet Joseph was at home. Joseph replied he was, whereupon the visitor said, 'I have brought you some flour and a ham.' Joseph arose and took the gift, and blessed the man in the name of the Lord. Turning to his wife, Emma, he said, 'I knew the Lord would answer my prayer.'[80] Joseph Smith was one who learned how to give and how to receive throughout his life."

CHAPTER 7

HULOPO'E BEACH

"The fight against Satan and his forces is not a little skirmish with a half-willed antagonist, but a battle royal with an enemy so powerful, entrenched, and organized that we are likely to be vanquished if we are not strong, well-trained, and watchful."[81]

- President Spencer W. Kimball

The following week was full of excitement as we conducted the first convert baptismal service on the island of Lāna'i in seven years. We met Randy Fernandez on a follow-up visit to a home where we'd left a *Book of Mormon* while tracting. We had left the book with Randy's wife, and she answered the door on our return visit. We asked if she had read from the *Book of Mormon*. She replied that she hadn't. However, as we were talking with her, Randy rushed to the door holding up the book, and asked, "Are you the ones who left this?"

"Yes," Elder Balane said. "Have you read it?"

"I've been reading through it all week and I want to know more," he said, excitement shining in his eyes.

We began teaching him the first discussion right then. As we shared the story of the first vision, the Spirit descended upon all of us. When we concluded the story, we asked Randy how he felt. He tried to describe the feelings of the Spirit but struggled to find the words.

"These feelings are a witness from the Holy Spirit," I told him. The Spirit again descended upon us as a witness to my words.

Randy looked at us with awe, "I know that what you shared is true. I know Joseph Smith is a prophet."

Randy was eager to learn as much as he could. We taught each of the lessons quickly, and he began attending church each week. He finished reading the *Book of Mormon*, and we gave him a triple combination so he could read the *Doctrine and Covenants* and *Pearl of Great Price*. It was only three weeks from our first meeting to his baptismal service. There is no font on the island, so the service was held on the beach, and the baptism was performed in the ocean.

Randy asked me to perform the baptism, which was an experience I will always cherish. It's an honor and privilege to exercise the power and authority of the priesthood. The first baptism I performed was on O'ahu for a Polynesian man who weighed more than three hundred pounds. I wanted to make sure I got him under the water completely, so I dipped him down rather quickly, causing water to splash over the glass surrounding the font and getting the observers in the front row wet. I wouldn't have this problem with Randy, as he weighed less than one hundred fifty pounds.

On Sunday, Randy was given the Aaronic priesthood and ordained to the office of a priest. He had the opportunity to exercise his newly received priesthood as he broke the bread and offered the sacramental prayer. The words of the prayer penetrated my soul. Tears flowed down my cheeks as Randy humbly spoke with the power of the Spirit.

Elder Balane and I were on a spiritual high as we met Manu on Monday afternoon. Manu greeted us with his signature "Aloha," and a spirit-filled hug. We talked about Randy's baptismal service and ordination to the priesthood as we drove.

After about fifteen minutes of driving, Manu asked, "Have you been to the resort where Randy works?"

"No," I said. "We've always met him at his home. I wanted to see the resort, but we haven't had time to make the twenty-mile round trip bike ride."

"Well, there it is," Manu said as he pointed out the window.

"Have we already gone ten miles?" I asked.

"Travel is much faster with paved roads, which you have learned are rare on Lāna'i. There are only thirty miles of paved roads, and today, we've used ten of them," Manu answered.

As I looked at the spectacular grounds and buildings of the resort complex, I asked, "Are you going to take us to see the resort?"

"No," Manu answered. "You can learn and experience more surrounded by God's creations."

We could see the beautiful resort in the distance as we drove past. It looked like a place reserved for the rich and famous. I was curious about the price. "What does a room cost per night?" I asked.

"The hotel rooms start at $650 per night, and the luxury suites cost $11,000 a night," Manu said.

I was expecting it to be expensive, but those numbers didn't seem real. I received less than $200 a month to pay for my food, clothing, toiletries, and anything else I needed. With a gallon of milk and a box of Honey Nut Cheerios costing me $16 on Lāna‘i, I thought a bowl of cereal was a luxury.

Shortly after we passed the resort, we saw a large rock on the right side of the road with "Hulopo‘e Beach Park" printed in yellow capital letters on it. We pulled into a small parking lot. For the first time on one of our Monday expeditions, we were actually on asphalt, and there were other vehicles around. We walked ten yards from the parking lot through a small group of palm trees. We were greeted by the spectacular expanse of pearl-white sand and sparkling blue water. Small, white-crested waves rolled onto the beach. They wrapped around the long, crescent-shaped bay, framed by a sea cliff to the west and lava rocks to the east.

The 217-room resort within walking distance and paved roads from Lāna‘i City made this beach park—with its picnic tables, showers, barbecue grills, and restrooms—the most visited beach on the island. However, Hulopo‘e Beach was rarely crowded. Most of the time, it was much like today, with a couple dozen people spread across the beach.

"Welcome to Hulopo‘e Beach," Manu said. "Hulopo‘e is one of the best places in the world to snorkel, as you will see a wide assortment of fish, sea turtles, a healthy coral reef system, and spinner dolphins. The dolphins frequently come into the bay and enjoy swimming with those who are snorkeling and swimming."

We followed Manu as he walked toward the east end of the beach. We stopped where the sand ended at a lava flow that went into the ocean to form large tide pools. A quick scan of the tide pools revealed an array of fish swimming in them. Manu had brought with him a small bucket. He walked through the tide pool, reached into the water, and grabbed something out. He placed what he'd captured into the bucket and put on a lid.

Manu walked back to us with the bucket. "I have something I would like to show you."

Manu set it on the ground and removed the lid. We peered into the bucket and saw a small crab. We watched as the crab struggled to climb from his prison. After exerting some effort, the crab was able to pull himself out and escape. Before the crab got too far, Manu grabbed him, placed him back into the bucket and returned the lid. Manu slowly walked through the tide pools, the water swishing around his lower legs and grazing the edges of his shorts. He gazed into the liquid pools around the rocks and then bent down and again grabbed something and placed it into the bucket. After a few more minutes of searching, Manu reached into the ocean and placed another item into the bucket. When he returned, he set the bucket on the ground in front of us and removed the lid. We looked inside to see three small crabs.

We watched as the crabs struggled to climb out of the bucket. When one crab began to climb, the other two crabs would grab the escaping crab and pull him back to the bottom. The crabs never learned; they continually pulled each other back into the bucket.

"Individually, the crabs could easily escape," Manu said. "But once you have two or more crabs in the bucket, the lid is not necessary. They prevent each other from escaping. Hawaiians have observed this phenomenon for centuries; however, this is not a phenomenon unique to crabs or to Hawai'i. In Hawai'i, we refer to those who criticize and pull down others as crabs.

"I believe the crab mentality is a result of envy. Envy is a form of pride that focuses on what we don't have. It's the attitude, 'If I can't have it, neither can you.' Envy is pointed at what another person has and desires to spoil it. Envy is an urge to destroy what is good in another. Envy is born out of the pain of emptiness. Envy cannot tolerate the fullness of someone else's cup, so it seeks to destroy a full cup to restore balance, ensuring that all cups are empty. Destructive envy represents an urgent need to spoil in order to remove the pain of lack.[82] Common manifestations of envy are criticism, faultfinding, backbiting, and gossiping to pull down others."

"Like Joseph's brothers in the Old Testament," Elder Balane said.

"Exactly," Manu agreed. "This is a classic example of envy. Joseph's brothers envied his coat of many colors, his relationship with their father, and his gift of dreams. To eliminate their perceived pain of lack, his brothers, 'moved with envy, sold Joseph into Egypt.'[83]

"Another example comes from Richard Paul Evans, a successful LDS author. While working as an advertising executive, Richard Paul Evans wrote a book for his children in his spare time called *The Christmas Box*. He self-published the book and sold millions of copies, eventually selling the book rights to the publisher Simon & Schuster for $4.2 million," Manu said, squatting down in front of the bucket and gently stroking the back of one of the crabs. "Richard Paul Evans said this about his success, 'It is a common social phenomenon that members of a group will attempt to "pull down" any individual member who achieves success beyond the others... It is arguable that America is becoming a giant crab pot. Instead of being inspired by others' success, small-minded people (and this represents a significant percentage of the population) resent others' achievements because they fear that they are being left behind...My wife and I experienced the effects of crab mentality firsthand. With the success of my first book, *The Christmas Box*, our world changed in some negative ways that we did not expect. Friends stopped talking to us, family stopped visiting, false rumors were spread through our neighborhood about us. It was a difficult time, one that required a lot of forgiving. When I told my father about what was happening to us, he wisely replied, 'You have to understand that your success will always remind others of their failures.'"[84]

Manu stood and looked me in the eye. Then he turned his penetrating gaze on Elder Balane. "I, too, have personally experienced the crab mentality," he said. "One time I remember well was when I was in college. I'd learned how to speed read and I often had classmates inquire how I succeeded even though I spent less time studying than they did. I would tell them I could speed read, expecting them to ask how they, too, might acquire the skill. Instead, they'd become angry with me and wouldn't talk to me anymore. I was called into the dean's office twice during my senior year because some of my classmates reported me as a cheater. I explained to the dean that I had worked every day for three years to increase my reading speed. I told him I could now do the same amount of studying I did as a sophomore in a fraction of the time. My meetings with the dean were brief, as there was no evidence of cheating—just false accusations. While there was no evidence of cheating, there was plenty of evidence of the crab mentality. Instead of trying to pull themselves up, they focused on pulling me down. In reality, I should not have been called into the dean's office for cheating. Instead, it should have been my classmates who were called in for lying, slander, backbiting, and gossiping. I didn't recognize it as crab mentality at the time, but I see it clearly now. Looking back, I wish I'd had an understanding of the crab mentality in college because it would have been very helpful in understanding and dealing with this situation."

"Wow. Envy is much more prevalent than I would have ever guessed," I said, shaking my head.

"That it is," Manu said. He walked up beside me and clapped a hand on my shoulder. "Unfortunately, you will find the crab mentality everywhere—even among the members of the Lord's church. Hopefully, there is less envy among the saints; however, President Benson taught that envy is the most common form of pride. He said, 'Most of us consider pride to be a sin of those on the top, such as the rich and the learned, looking down at the rest of us. There is, however, a far more common ailment among us—and that is pride from the bottom looking up. It is manifest in so many ways, such as faultfinding, gossiping, backbiting, murmuring, living beyond our means, envying, coveting, withholding gratitude and praise that might lift another, and being unforgiving and jealous.'[85]

"Elders, if either of you are ever called to serve as a bishop, remember this principle," Manu said. "It's often the person who is bringing you a complaint who needs to be met with, not the person they are complaining about. Don't make the same mistake as my college dean and call the wrong person into your office. Understanding envy and the crab mentality can help you discern who it is you need to meet with.

"Envy can show up anywhere," Manu warned. "Even at a ward pinewood derby. A few years ago, I was involved with a pinewood derby where one boy's car easily won every race. I heard several of the other boys call this boy a cheater. I approached them and explained that instead of trying to pull him down with false accusations of cheating, they should learn what he did to make his car fast. He obviously did things they did not do.

"A year following this experience, one of my friend's sons won the pinewood derby in St. George, Utah. I asked him what they did to win, and he said he bought a book on how to create a fast car and followed the instructions. I asked him how many people at the pinewood derby asked him how his family had built a fast car. He responded, 'You are the first.' I then asked how many people accused him and his son of cheating and he answered, 'Several.'"

"That's so sad," I said, shaking my head.

Manu sighed. "Yes. It is very sad, but it is true. When you strive for excellence, don't be surprised by those who will try to pull you down. Just recognize it for what it is and keep on climbing. Don't let the crab mentality of others stop you from growing and achieving.

"If you ever find yourself trying to pull down another, remember this: the achievement of another in no way limits or takes away from your achievement. The more you can develop an abundance mentality, the more you will be genuinely happy for the successes, well-being, achievements, recognition, and good fortune of other people. You'll recognize that their success adds to—rather than detracts from—your life.[86] The more you develop an abundance mentality, the less envy you'll feel."

Manu tipped the bucket on its side and set the crabs free into the tide pools. "Let's go sit in the shade of the palm trees, and I'll share with you another dream I had."[87]

I smiled, excited to learn more from Manu. We walked a short distance to a group of palm trees and found a comfortable place to sit in the sand. Manu waited until we were settled and silent.

"One of the most extreme examples of pride and envy is found in Lucifer, the son of the morning," Manu said. "This dream helped me understand that envy is one of the drivers of Satan's destructive behavior.

"At the start of the dream, I was in a go-kart race. These go-karts were agile and quick, yet they were so small, the racers had a hard time fitting into them. Their knees and elbows protruded awkwardly from the top and sides of the carts. The track that we raced on and the scenery around it was beautiful: flowers, streams, waterfalls, mountains, and hills. There were parts of the track that included rough terrain where we'd have to travel over logs and through water. At one point, I crashed and went off the track. However, I was able to return to the track and continue the race. I eventually crossed the finish line. The vast majority of racers finished ahead of me, with only a few finishing behind me.

"There was a scene from the dream that replayed in my mind until I awoke. A friend I played soccer with in high school and a group of his friends were trying to persuade me to get a tattoo. They each had the tattoo and were persistent in trying to convince me to get the same tattoo, even though I told them I didn't want it. As I continued to refuse the tattoo, they began giving me the tattoo. The tattoo was of a go-kart, and under the go-kart were the words 'Unum Pluris Anima.' I didn't know the meaning of the words, and my friends didn't explain it to me. They were acting like the tattoo was not a big deal; like it was the cool thing to do. After finishing the tattoo, my friends changed. I had the feeling that I'd been tricked.

"When I awoke from the dream, I had the feeling that this was an inspired dream from the Lord, so I recorded it. My brother, who has the gift to interpret dreams, worked with me to receive an interpretation. After pondering, studying, and much prayer, the meaning of the dream was revealed."

I leaned toward Manu, fascinated and eager to hear his explanation of the dream. Elder Balane did the same.

"The go-kart is symbolic of life, with the race symbolic of the race of life," Manu said. "The beautiful scenery and the race track represent that life is beautiful. The smallness of the cart is symbolic of the fact that our mature, infinite, and eternal spirits are contained in finite, mortal bodies. The finish line is symbolic of death. The fact that I was one of the last racers to cross the finish line represents that we are in the final moments of the last days. The go-kart tattoo was placed on my buttocks. This represents the fact that Satan does much of his work in secret and hiding in his attempts to deceive people.

"We discovered that 'Unum Pluris Anima' was Latin for 'One More Soul.' When my brother and I first heard these words, chills went down our spines. The phrase 'One More Soul' brings a frightening realization that Satan has a well-orchestrated army and proven methodology to win souls. Satan and his minions are actively seeking the next soul to destroy. They are damned souls who are driven by pride to spoil and destroy for others what they know they can never have for themselves. Envy drives Satan to seek 'that all men might be miserable like unto himself.'"[88]

"Wow," I said under my breath as the imagery of the dream and its interpretation sank in. I wouldn't have guessed the meaning behind the go-karts and tattoo, but once Manu explained the symbolism, it was so simple.

"To Satan, a person is a quest to satisfy his destructive envy," Manu said. "It's just another number to chalk up on his list. A soul won by Satan is the end, as light, truth, and progression are destroyed. They are damned. There is nothing left for Satan and his minions to do, but to destroy 'One More Soul.' In stark contrast, a soul won to Christ is just the beginning. Those who choose God will grow in light and truth. They will add to God's glory and creation. God says, 'the worth of a soul is great.' God creates value and worth. Satan's sole object is to destroy it.

"We must fight to win souls to Christ prior to the second coming. Satan is fighting hard and winning too many souls to his side. The war in Heaven 'is continued in mortality in the conflict between right and wrong, between the gospel and false principles. The same contestants and the same issues are doing battle, and the same salvation is at stake.'[89] The battle for souls continues.

"We know Christ wins the war prior to His second coming. This fact causes some to mistakenly think that, since Christ wins, they don't need to worry. Christ won the war in Heaven, but the war was not to determine who will win (that was known in the preexistence and it is also known that Christ will win at the second coming). The war will determine whose side you and your friends are on. We must fight to ensure as many as possible are on the Lord's side. We mourned over every soul that was lost to Satan in the preexistence. In fact, we even mourned greatly over Satan. Joseph Smith recorded his vision of the casting out of Satan, saying, 'And this we saw...that an angel of God who was in authority in the presence of God, who rebelled against the Only Begotten Son whom the Father loved, and who was in the bosom of the Father, was thrust down from the presence of God and the Son, and was called Perdition, for the heavens wept over him—he was Lucifer, a son of the morning.'[90] Our efforts are critical, for we will mourn for each soul lost to Satan at the Lord's second coming."

"My father taught me that many people follow Satan unknowingly," Elder Balane interjected.

Manu nodded in agreement. "Yes, he creates an illusion and a mirage that fools many. He is cunning and crafty and works in the shadows."

"Why can't people see through it?" I asked, frustrated at the truth of Manu's words.

"That's a good question, Elder Taylor," Manu said. "I will answer your question with a story. One day, while walking down the street, a highly successful business woman was tragically hit by a bus and killed. Her soul arrived at the pearly gates and she was met by Peter.

"'Welcome to the Gates of Heaven,' said Peter. 'To determine where you will spend eternity, we're going to have you spend a day in Hell and a day in Heaven. After these visits, you will choose your destiny.'

"'Actually, I think I've made up my mind. I prefer to stay in Heaven,' said the woman.

"'Sorry, but before your decision can be made you must first visit Hell,' answered Peter.

"Peter placed the executive in an elevator, which descended a great distance before coming to a stop. The doors opened and she found herself stepping onto a beautiful golf course. In the distance was a country club, and standing in front of her were many of her friends. They were all dressed in evening gowns and cheering for her. They ran up and kissed her on both cheeks and talked about old times. They played a wonderful round of golf. That night they went to the country club and she enjoyed an excellent steak and lobster dinner. She met Lucifer, who was a really nice, handsome guy. She had a great time telling jokes and dancing. She was having such a good time that, before she knew it, it was time to leave. Everybody shook her hand and waved good-bye as she got on the elevator.

"The elevator went up and up and up. The doors opened at the pearly gates with Peter waiting for her. 'Now it's time to spend a day in Heaven,' he said.

"She spent the next twenty-four hours in Heaven and had a lovely, peaceful time. She got to explore beautiful plants and rivers, see old friends and family members, and marvel at the beautiful creations around her. She was surrounded by love and light, angelic music and all her ancestors. When her time was up, Peter came for her.

"'So, you've spent a day in Hell and you've spent a day in Heaven. Now you must choose your eternity,' he said.

"The woman paused for a second and replied, 'Well, I never thought I'd say this, I mean, Heaven was amazing, but I think I had a better time in Hell.'

"'Peter escorted her to the elevator and again she went down to Hell. When the doors of the elevator opened, she found herself standing in a desolate wasteland covered in garbage and filth. She saw her friends dressed in rags. Lucifer came up to her and put his arm on her shoulder. 'I don't understand,' stammered the woman. 'Yesterday, I was here and there was a golf course and a country club. We ate lobster, danced, and had a great time. Now all I see is a wasteland of garbage, and my friends look miserable.'

"Lucifer looked into her eyes and, with an evil smile replied, 'Yesterday, we were recruiting you; today you are one of us.'"

Manu paused and looked from Elder Balane to me, peering into our eyes as if making sure his message had sunk in. Without him speaking the question aloud, I nodded my head. I understood.

"Satan works very hard to make evil look enticing and fun, and to make that which is good appear dull and boring," Manu said. "The prophet Isaiah warns us, saying, 'Woe unto them that call evil good, and good evil; that put darkness for light, and light for darkness; that put bitter for sweet, and sweet for bitter!'[91] You must always be on guard against the fiery darts of the adversary. Anyone can fall victim to the deceptions of Satan—even the very elect.[92]

Manu rose to his feet and began walking along the beach, Elder

Balane and I on each side. "Take a look at each of the people you see," Manu said as we walked, gesturing to the small clusters of people around us. "They are our brothers and sisters. Will they be on the Lord's side? The work we do as missionaries—to bring people to Christ—is very important as we prepare for His second coming."

We walked in silence along the beach, through the palm trees and back to Manu's truck. I was filled with the Spirit, testifying to the truth of the lessons Manu had taught. I could feel the echoes of the pain I'd felt in the preexistence when my brothers and sisters were cast out, following the war in Heaven. Tears spilled down my cheeks as I remembered how I wept with sadness in that premortal realm. I could tangibly feel the pain and sadness I was going to experience for the lost souls at the second coming. It was impressed upon me how important it was to stay on the Lord's side; and to keep my family and friends on the Lord's side.

CHAPTER 8

KEŌMOKU CHURCH

"The most important knowledge in the world is gospel knowledge."[93]

- President Joseph Fielding Smith

In my weekly letter to the mission president, I requested to stay in Lāna'i for the six months I had remaining as a full-time missionary. I'd grown to love the members of the branch, and the many individuals we were teaching about the good news of Jesus Christ. I wanted to continue to learn from Manu and the ancient sites of Lāna'i. However, I knew that even with six more months on the island, I wouldn't be able to learn all the wisdom Manu had to share. As much as I wished the mission president would grant my request, I had the feeling as I wrote the letter that my time on Lāna'i was coming to an end.

After completing our P-day chores, we arrived at Lāna'i High and Elementary at the appointed time. We parked our bikes outside of Manu's classroom and entered. Manu was meeting with a student, but motioned for us to come to his desk. He introduced us to the student and greeted us with a hug. Manu assisted the student for a few more minutes and then shared some parting words of encouragement as the student left for the day.

As we followed Manu to his truck, he said, "I'd love to take you back to Hulopo'e Beach to swim with the dolphins, but I know that's not allowed as a missionary. You'll have to return to Lāna'i following your missionary service. Then I can take you swimming with the dolphins, cliff jumping, snorkeling, and fishing. It would also give us time to see the sites we won't have time to visit on your P-days."

I nodded, eager to take him up on the suggestion. "That sounds like a great idea," I said.

"I would come back just for one of your wife's delicious meals," Elder Balane agreed.

Manu laughed. "You are welcome to eat at our home anytime," he said. He pulled his truck out of the school parking lot and onto the main road. "Today, we're headed to the town of Keōmoku. It was a small fishing village of one to two hundred people until 1899 when the Maunalei Sugar Company was started and hundreds of workers came to work in the sugarcane fields. The company built a large community with houses, stores, an inn, a sugar mill, a pier, a railroad, and a hospital. The sugar company appeared to be thriving, and the village grew to be the population center of the island, with around two thousand people. However, the life of the sugar company was short lived. In 1900, many of the plantation workers died from exposure to a plague, and the freshwater sources used to irrigate the fields turned salty. These events forced the sugar company to close in 1901. With its closing, the population dropped dramatically and continued to decline through the 1950s as residents moved to Lāna'i City."

Manu pulled his truck to the side of the road. There didn't appear to be anything around for miles. I looked around. "Where is Keōmoku?"

"This is it," answered Manu. "Little evidence of the sugar industry and village remains."

We got out of the truck and walked down a small trail surrounded by trees. I looked ahead and saw a beautiful wooden church nestled beneath a group of coconut trees. As my eyes connected with the church, I was warmed by the Holy Spirit.

"Welcome to Ka Lanakila o Ka Malamalama," Manu said, his hand sweeping through the air toward the building ahead of us. "This church was built in 1903, and church services were held here until 1951. This is the last wooden structure existing from the village. Recently the twenty-four by forty-foot church was restored to preserve this important piece of Lāna'i history."

"Can we go inside?" I asked.

"Yes," Manu said. Then he hesitated. "But remember, this is a house of God. This building was dedicated to the Lord by the island kupuna (elders) to be a place of worship. While Keōmoku has been abandoned, God and His blessings never left this place. The dedicatory prayer and blessings pronounced on this chapel are eternal."

I approached the small porch on the front of the church. As I took the first stair leading to the open door of the church, I heard a small voice whisper, "He." I paused for a moment, not expecting to hear a voice. I took the second step and heard the word, "who." I heard one word as I slowly took each of the remaining four steps: "Has. Eyes. To. See."

I stopped on the small square covered porch. "Many who come here only see an old building," I thought. "But those who have eyes to see connect with God and receive His power, spirit, grace, and knowledge." As I prayed in preparation to enter the church, I heard the words, "He who has ears to hear, let him enter."

When I walked through the front door, I was wrapped in the same warmth I felt when I first laid eyes on the church. There were four rectangular windows symmetrically spaced on each side wall. The windows contained no glass or covering, but were open to the outside. On the opposite side of the front door was the pulpit, with a rectangular window on each side. There were no wooden benches or chairs in the church. The single rectangular room was empty and open except for the pulpit. Hanging on the wall behind the pulpit was a plaque that read:

Ua la'a No Iehova
Ka Lanakila o Ka Malamalama
Hoolaaia
October 4, 1903

"Manu, what does the plaque say?" I asked.

Manu answered, "'Ua la'a No Iehova' means, 'Sanctified for Jehovah' while 'Hoolaaia' refers to a ceremony and blessing to consecrate and make sacred. The plaque is pronouncing that this church was dedicated and consecrated to the Lord Jehovah on October 4, 1903.

"So what does the middle phrase 'Ka Lanakila o Ka Malamalama' mean?"

"Before I answer that question, there's something I'd like to teach you," Manu said. He motioned Elder Balane over so he could hear, too. "Principles can be broken into two categories: principles of knowledge and principles of skill. Principles of knowledge are things we know and believe, such as agency, justification, and grace. Principles of skill are things we know, believe, and do, such as repentance, fasting, and prayer.

"Distinguishing between principles of knowledge and principles of skill is extremely important because it determines how the principle is taught and how it is to be learned. With principles of knowledge, there are no 'hows' to be learned.

"Many people try to treat principles of knowledge as principles of skill and become frustrated when they can't apply them in daily life. They complain that the ideas are too abstract and of no benefit. They want to learn something they can do. They don't realize that knowledge is one of the most important possessions for living with Aloha.

"Principles of knowledge are something we 'know' not something we 'do.' The way one applies principles of knowledge is by understanding and believing them, and they most certainly affect how you live."

Manu walked behind the podium. Elder Balane and I stood in the center of the room with our eyes fixed on Manu as he taught.

"What if someone asked, 'How can I apply the grace of Christ in my everyday life?'" Manu asked. "The person may get frustrated when you can't give him a specific answer. It's not that there isn't a good answer. It's a bad question. You can't directly do things to apply Christ's grace in your life. You apply the grace of Christ by understanding it and believing it. You can know the grace of Christ, but you can't do the grace of Christ. However, understanding and believing in Christ's grace will change your life. When a person understands, and believes in Christ's grace, he's filled with hope and relies on the merits of Christ, and not his own. If you look deeply at the principles of knowledge, you can see how a knowledge and belief in them changes behavior and are thus applied by simply knowing them.

"An example can be found in Nazi Germany. Hitler believed the races were graded. There were, according to him, superior races and inferior races. According to Hitler, the highest race was the Aryan race—the race destined to be masters. The lowest races were the Jews and Blacks—those who, in Hitler's view, were the root of all of civilization's evils and ills.[94] From Hitler's belief in graded races, can we predict his behavior?"

Elder Balane nodded, "Yes, and history documents the destruction his beliefs caused."

"Was Hitler's knowledge in accordance with eternal principles?" Manu asked.

"Obviously not," Elder Balane said. "Hitler's actions, driven by his beliefs, resulted in much destruction and eventually led to his death."

"What would have been the key to transforming Hitler's behaviors?" Manu turned his penetrating gaze on me.

"If he didn't believe in a superior race," I said.

"Exactly," Manu said, giving me a pleased smile. "It would

have been to change his belief in graded races to a belief that all men are created equal. President Boyd K. Packer taught, 'True doctrine, understood, changes attitudes and behavior. The study of the doctrines of the gospel will improve behavior more quickly than a study of behavior will improve behavior...That is why we stress so forcefully the study of the doctrines of the gospel.'[95]

"Learning principles of knowledge, such as grace, justification, sanctification, and other doctrines of the gospel are extremely important because they change the way we live. As we understand and believe true doctrines, we will be more Christlike—filled with greater joy and happiness. We will live with greater Aloha.

"With this explanation, I think you will see the power contained in the phrase, 'Ka Lanakila o Ka Malamalama.'" Manu pointed to the plaque behind him. "The direct translation to English is 'The Triumph of Knowledge.' However, malamalama does not mean any knowledge—it is knowledge of light and truth—it is gospel knowledge.

"The principle of knowledge I'm going to talk about today is one of the key reasons why Hawai'i is consistently ranked as the least stressed and happiest state in America. It is a principle that many people in the mainland—and especially Utah—need to learn. While Hawai'i is the least stressed of the fifty states, Utah has consistently ranked as one of the top five most stressful states in America.[96] When you truly understand this Aloha principle, your life will be transformed.

"The ancient Hawaiian language contains no past or future tenses. All language is present tense. We are eternal beings with no beginning and no end. There is no past. There is no future. All things are present. Hawaiians understand that time is an illusion. The Lord himself declares, 'All things are present before mine eyes.'[97] One of the reasons ancient Hawaiians did not keep a written history was because it created a past. Living in the present is one of the keys to joyful living—one of the keys to a life of Aloha. Life is to be enjoyed in each moment of now. The idea of a past and a future is a temporary illusion of mortality.

"One of my favorite scriptures is 'Men are that they might have joy.'[98] The words 'are' and 'have' are present tense. We are to have joy now. Joy is not a future state to achieve. Joy is not a reward to receive after years of work or a gift reserved for the next life. We are to experience the glad tidings of great joy now. To enjoy the present, you must let go of the pains and guilt of the past and eliminate the worries of the future. The Lord teaches in the Sermon on the Mount, 'Take therefore no thought for the morrow: for the morrow shall take thought for the things of itself.'[99] This is a scripture that's confusing to some; but, it's easy to understand when you know how to live in the present. Another translation of this verse reads, 'So don't be anxious about tomorrow. God will take care of your tomorrow too. Live one day at a time.'[100]

"A Hawaiian proverb states, 'The path to God is a simple one of joy.' God created you to have joy. Joy is innate in you. It is when you live with joy that you fulfill the measure of your creation.

"Last year I was working on a new book and took a trip to a mountain cabin to write.[101] The first days there were amazing, as I spent time with God, received revelation, communed with angels, and wrote by inspiration. One evening, several days into the trip, I was hit with temptations. I initially resisted and discarded the temptations; however, Satan didn't give up and the temptations continued to bombard me. My thoughts and actions led me to start taking steps toward giving in to those temptations. Thankfully, I discerned what was happening, and I cast Satan and his temptations out. I began to feel great disappointment in both my thoughts and my actions. I messed up and felt that I was in no position to write. I even had the thought that I should end the trip and return home in the morning. If I'd lost the Spirit of the Lord, there would be no point in staying the remaining days. I was in no mood to write, so I began reading from the many books I'd brought with me to the cabin. After about an hour of reading, I retired to bed early. I knelt next to the bed to pray and asked the Lord to forgive me. After my prayer, I pulled back the covers, climbed into bed, and went to sleep.

"That night I received a dream from the Lord unlike other dreams I've received from Him. The dream was a seven-word statement that was repeated again and again. Throughout the night, the Lord spoke the words I needed to hear: 'Don't let the past steal your present.' When I arose, these words were ingrained in my mind and I wrote them down."

"We have a natural tendency to give up or quit when we make a mistake. Satan whispers lies into our ears to fill us with guilt, doubt, and despair. I had thoughts of going home and giving up on writing for the week. I'd messed up. How could I possibly continue?

"Mercifully, the message from the Lord was, 'Don't let the past steal your present. Just because you made a mistake yesterday, it doesn't have to affect what you do today. It's a new day. It's the present. Today you can live in My presence, receive My forgiveness, and continue on in the work of writing. I am quick to forgive, uplift, and bless, and I will help you along the path until you shall be crowned with glory on high and take your seat in the heavens with Me and My Father.' I accepted His grace and was again caught up in His presence and filled with His spirit and direction. I resumed writing. I was not going to let the past steal my present.

"The Hawaiian word for sin is 'hala,' which means 'to miss.' Hala is similar to the Greek word for sin, 'hamarita.' In Greek, 'hamarita' is an archery term meaning 'miss the mark.' Elder Taylor, how many attempts will Jesus give you to hit the mark?"

I wasn't ready for the question so it took me a minute to answer. "I don't know. A lot."

"Elder Balane?" Manu asked, turning to him.

Elder Balane smiled, unsure. "As many as we need?"

Manu chuckled. "Yes, Elder Balane. He will give you as many as you need. Whether you need ten tries or ten thousand tries, the Lord will always be with you. Jesus declares, 'I will never leave you nor forsake you.'[102]

"When you miss the target, you repent, grab an arrow, and try again. Jesus wants you to try until you hit the target. Don't let your previously missed shot prevent you from taking the next one. Don't let the past steal your present. The apostle Paul wrote, 'This one thing I do, forgetting those things which are behind...I press toward the mark.'[103] The prophet Jeremiah declared, 'Hope returns when I remember this one thing: The Lord's unfailing love and mercy still continue, fresh as the morning, as sure as the sunrise.'[104]

"As we live, we're going to miss the target. We learn to become like Jesus the way a child learns to walk—they fall hundreds and hundreds of times. Elder Taylor, how many attempts will you give your children to walk?"

"As many as they need," I answered, knowing the answer now.

"Of course," Manu said. "As parents, we don't condemn or get angry with our children when they fall. We know this is a part of the process of learning to walk. We encourage them. We celebrate the progress they make and encourage them to get up and continue on. As a parent, would there ever be a point when you would say, 'You've fallen 532 times. That's it. You're done. I'm not helping you anymore. I give up. You will never learn to walk. You have failed.' Ridiculous, right? Satan tries to get us to believe this very thing, though—that if we sin or make a mistake, our Heavenly Father will be angry with us, condemn and punish us, and leave us. As we understand that He is our Father and wants us to learn to become like Him, we realize that He's like the parent helping his child learn to walk. He will encourage us. He will celebrate our efforts and progress. He will stay with us until we hit the mark.

"Oftentimes, when a child falls down, they'll laugh, hop up, and try again. In our quest to become like Jesus, we're going to fall many times. We're going to sin repeatedly as we're learning, growing, and getting better. When we miss the target, Jesus doesn't condemn us. He's not mad at us. He simply says, 'Try again. Try until you do hit the target.'"

"Satan wants us to give up. The Lord wants us to grab another arrow and try again," I said, marveling at the simplicity.

"Exactly," Manu said. "Don't let a previous fall prevent you from taking the next step. You take that next shot, knowing you might miss again. The child takes that next step knowing they will fall again. As they practice, they improve their balance and begin to walk farther and farther without failing. You must crawl before you walk, and you must walk before you run. We are designed to learn by making mistakes.

"In the church, we often talk about the gospel of Jesus Christ. So, what exactly is the gospel of Jesus Christ? The word 'gospel' is derived from a word meaning 'good news' or 'glad tidings.' So, what is this good news?

"A part of this good news is found in Romans 5:8, 'While we were yet sinners, Christ died for us.' We will sin and miss the mark daily as we learn during the test of mortality, and yet we are in a saved condition through the redeeming blood of Jesus Christ. Jesus does not wait for us to reach perfection to save us. He saves us while we are sinners. We are not called Saints because we are righteous, but because we are sinners who keep trying.

"Forgiveness and salvation are not gifts to be received in the future. They are gifts the Lord wants us to receive in the present. During His earthly ministry, Jesus never said, "Your sins will be forgiven." He often used the present tense, "Your sins are forgiven."[105] There is power in declaring 'I am saved' in the present tense instead of 'I will be saved' or 'I hope to be saved.'

"When Christ came to the home of Zacchaeus, a short man who

climbed a sycamore tree to see Jesus, he said, 'This day is salvation come to this house...For the Son of man is come to seek and to save that which was lost.'[106] Christ wants you to accept the gift of salvation today, not in the future or after you're dead. Elders, has salvation come to your home? Can you say, 'I am saved?'"

I was silent as I considered his question.

"I think I can say it," Elder Balane said. But he sounded unsure.

"Isn't it arrogant or prideful to say 'I am saved?'" I asked.

"Why would you think it's prideful?" Manu asked.

"Well, how can we know for sure if we've been good enough to go to the celestial kingdom?"

"You're using the wrong criteria to determine whether you're saved," Manu said. He walked from behind the podium to stand in front of us. "If the criteria is 'Am I worthy to go to the celestial kingdom?' we would all be unworthy to enter. Perfection is the requirement for the celestial kingdom. We all have sinned and will continue to sin; therefore, we're imperfect and thus unworthy. Christ declares, 'For I the Lord cannot look upon sin with the least degree of allowance.'[107] To determine if we're going to the celestial kingdom, we must not ask, 'Am I worthy?' but 'Am I perfect in Christ?' We're not saved by our works or our perfection but by Christ's perfection. We're saved by Christ's merits, mercy, and grace. So, Elder Taylor, can you say, 'I am saved?'"

"I don't know," I answered, shaking my head.

"In the preexistence, did you wonder whether you would be cast out with Satan?" Manu asked.

I shrugged my shoulders.

"I don't remember the preexistence," Elder Balane said with a smile.

Manu smiled. "I don't think those who were on the Lord's side in the preexistence said, 'I sure hope I've been good enough to not be cast out with Lucifer. I sure hope I make it to earth. I don't know if I'm going to be cast out and I won't know until it happens.' Those who were on the Lord's side could say with confidence in the present tense, 'I am on the Lord's side. I am going to earth.'"

Elder Balane and I nodded our heads.

"Elder Taylor, we know you were on the Lord's side in the preexistence because you're here. As a result, we know that your resurrection is assured. There's nothing you can do on earth to lose your resurrection. In the preexistence, two-thirds of the hosts of Heaven kept their first estate and came to earth. Those who are born will be resurrected and receive a degree of glory, regardless of their actions on earth. They can't lose their first estate.

"Earth life is our second estate, a probationary state, a test. What is required to keep our second estate and be saved in the celestial kingdom? We must continue to choose Christ. We must be on the Lord's side. We must be perfect in Christ. When we're perfect in Christ, we can say with confidence, 'I am saved—I'm going to the celestial kingdom,' just as in the preexistence, those on the Lord's side could say with confidence, 'I am on the Lord's side. I'm going to earth.' If you choose Christ and accept His grace, you're saved now. So, Elder Taylor, can you say, 'I am saved?'

I frowned, confused. "Are you saying I am guaranteed the celestial kingdom?"

"Yes, if you endure to the end," Manu said.

"But earlier, you said I was saved *now*. So, can I be unsaved?"

"In the preexistence, a third of the hosts of Heaven were cast out with Satan," Manu said. "At any point prior to Satan being cast out, individuals could leave the Lord's side and join Satan's team—and, sadly, there were those who did. Likewise, while on earth, you must remain on the Lord's side until the end of earth life. Elder Bruce R. McConkie shared the following as to what is required to endure to the end: 'Everyone in the Church who is on the straight and narrow path, who is striving and struggling and desiring to do what is right, though is far from perfect in this life; if he passes out of this life while he's on the straight and narrow, he's going to go on to eternal reward in his Father's kingdom...If you are on that path when death comes because this is the time and the day appointed, this the probationary estate, you will never fall off from it; and for all practical purposes, your calling and election is made sure.'[108] So, Elder Taylor, can you now say, 'I am saved?'"

"I think so," I said.

Elder Balane laughed and smacked me on the back. "Come on, Elder. You can do it."

"Sadly, there are many in the church who know of the atoning sacrifice of Jesus Christ but have not received His good news: that they are saved and forgiven now and that they can enjoy this gift every hour of each day and can say with confidence, 'Christ has saved me.'" Manu paused and turned the full force of his gaze on me. His smile was gentle but his eyes were strong. "Elder Taylor, you need to say the words, 'I am saved,' out loud."

While I was still a little uncomfortable saying the words, I declared in a shaky voice, "I am saved." As I said the words, I was filled with a witness of the Spirit that this was true. I tried again, this time with more confidence. "I am saved."

"Yes. You are," Manu affirmed.

Tears of joy ran down my face. I gave Manu a hug of gratitude; the first time I'd initiated a hug in my life.

Manu pulled back to look in my face. "You are beginning to experience the joy of living in the present," he said. "There is an old Hawaiian saying that you can only live in paradise right now, for now is all there ever is. We should talk of salvation in the present tense, not as some event to take place in the future. Through your born again and covenant relationship with Christ, you become what the scriptures call 'perfect in Christ.'[109] Present tense. Satan wants you to believe his lie that, when you sin and make mistakes, you're lost, disconnected from God, and will never be enough. Satan wants you to feel despair and hopelessness. It is the whispering of Satan that claims 'you are not enough.' In Hawaiian, the word for 'enough' means 'connected to God' and 'not enough' means 'disconnected from God.' When you're 'perfect in Christ' you are connected with God. You're enough. You're saved. This is the good news of Jesus Christ."

Elder Balane stood. "Do I get a hug, too?"

"Of course," Manu said, extending his arms.

"I meant from Elder Taylor," Elder Balane said, laughing.

"Of course," I said. Elder Balane came in for a group hug. We pulled apart and turned our eyes back to the plaque hanging on the wall.

"Hawaiians believe that words have 'mana,' which means they

carry divine and spiritual power," Manu said. "There is great power in the words, 'I am saved.' However, to be fully understood, these words must be experienced, for they carry with them the power of Christ's love, grace, forgiveness, and perfection."

I knew exactly what he meant. I had just experienced the words, 'I am saved.'

"Manu, would it be okay for me to take a picture with the dedication plaque of the church to help me remember this day?" I asked.

Manu nodded his head, and I handed my camera to Elder Balane. I invited Manu to join me in the picture. Manu put his arm around my shoulder and we smiled for the camera. I took another picture of the exterior of the church before getting into the truck for the ride home.

That evening, I wrote in my journal these words: "I've been a member of The Church of Jesus Christ of Latter-day Saints for twenty years and have been a full-time missionary for over a year, and yet I had not fully received the good news of Jesus Christ. I will forever remember March 18, 1996, as the day I was able to declare, 'I am saved.' I will proclaim the good news of Jesus Christ to all who will listen, that they may also experience the joy, peace, and rejoicing that comes with the knowledge of salvation and living in the present.

CHAPTER 9

LĀNA'I COMMUNITY CEMETERY

"Life beyond the grave is as real and as certain as is our life here on earth."[110]

- President Thomas S. Monson

Our next P-day had arrived. As Elder Balane and I got on our bikes to head to the school, I had the thought that I should bring some tissues.

"Hold on a minute," I said, as I ran back into the apartment. I grabbed a pack of portable tissues and shoved them in the back pocket of my slacks. Elder Balane was already on his bike when I rejoined him outside. I quickly folded my right pant leg, stuffed it into my sock, and we were off. We pulled up to the school and parked our bikes in the usual spot in front of Manu's classroom. As we locked our bikes together, Manu walked out of the building and greeted us with his signature bear hug and Aloha.

"How was school today?" I asked.

"It was another wonderful day with people I love," Manu replied.

We piled into the truck and buckled in. As Manu settled behind the wheel, he chuckled softly. "There was a humorous story the third-grade teacher shared with me today," he said. "Her class was learning about Martin Luther King, Jr., and she gave her class the assignment to complete the phrase, 'I have a dream that one day...' One of her students completed the assignment with, 'I have a dream that one day handicapped people will be able to park wherever they want.'"

We all laughed. "I love being a teacher. Each day is a fun adventure," he said.

After a couple of minutes of driving, Manu pulled into a cemetery. This was the shortest drive he'd taken us on so far. It was on the outskirts of Lāna'i City. Manu drove slowly down the dirt roads of the cemetery. He turned down one of the rows and brought the truck to a stop.

"I come here at least once a week and, today, I thought I would have you join me," Manu said. When he climbed out of the truck, he paused and reached under his seat. He pulled out a well-worn, leather scripture case. Then he grabbed a bright and colorful lei made of real flowers from the top of his dashboard. He settled the lei around his neck and smiled at us.

We followed Manu, who strode toward a white, marble headstone with the confidence of someone who'd been here many times. We stood back as Manu knelt in the red dirt that surrounded the grave. I felt a desire to kneel as well and lowered myself to my knees near the grave. As I began to pray for Manu, Elder Balane knelt next to me. When I finished my short prayer, I watched Manu continue to pray. After a couple of minutes, Manu remained kneeling but raised his head. He took the lei from his neck and placed it on the headstone as he said, 'Aloha, my son. Aloha.'

Manu shifted from kneeling to sitting Indian style on the ground, and Elder Balane and I did the same. The name on the headstone read:

Mikela Jonathan Nāpela
March 23, 1980 - March 9, 1992

Manu unzipped his scripture case and pulled something from the pages of his Bible. As he did so, tears filled his eyes. Manu was not afraid to show his emotions, but this cry was different. You could feel his hurt, pain, and sorrow. "Mikela is my oldest son. I still miss him so much," he said, his voice cracking with emotion.

I handed Manu a tissue from my back pocket, and he handed me a few pages that had been torn from a 3 x 5-inch spiral notebook and stapled together. "Elder Taylor, will you please read this note aloud?" He asked, sniffing. "I don't think I will be able to read it clearly."

I looked at the hand-written note, unsure if I would make it through either. But I couldn't say no, so I began to read. "Mikela, I am on a bus right now and wanted to write you a letter. I've missed you while I've been away. I love playing games with you. You're an amazing son, and I'm very blessed to be your dad." I had to pause and clear my throat, blinking back tears. "Thank you for your obedience. I appreciate your help with chores, both inside and outside the house. Thank you for being a good older brother. Thank you also for being a good example for your brother and sister to learn from. They look up to you and like to be included in what you do, and they like when you play with them. You're a good leader and friend. You're a good learner, and I enjoy watching you improve and excel as you practice and grow. Basketball is one example of this. Success in basketball is like success in most things. It's the result of hard work, experience, and hundreds and hundreds of hours of practice. It's fantastic to see you read your scriptures every day on your own. The scriptures are a tremendous source of spiritual strength and power. Keep up the great work. You will be a great deacon, and you will be a great full-time missionary. Jesus Christ loves you. Jesus was crucified for your sins, and it's by Jesus's grace you are forgiven and saved. I Love You! Dad."

Manu held out his hand as I read the final words, and I handed him back the pages. Tears streamed down his cheeks. "My son never became a deacon," he said softly. "My son will not serve a full-time mission. He was killed a couple weeks before his twelfth birthday. He was hit by a car as he rode his bike around the neighborhood. The day of his twelfth birthday was one of the hardest days of my life. The pain was so great, I thought my heart would burst. I wondered if the tears and pain would ever stop."

The raw emotion on Manu's face had reduced Elder Balane and me to tears, as well. We sat quietly, listening to his story.

"In the midst of my tears, I heard a voice say, 'Go to your son's room and get his scriptures.'" Manu wiped his nose with the tissue I'd given him. "I ignored the voice at first, as I knew entering his room would bring a flood of memories, and with those memories would come more pain and tears. After the third prompting from the

Spirit, I slowly walked into his room. As I entered, I saw his scriptures sitting on his desk. His room had remained unchanged in the weeks since his passing, and his scriptures sat where he had last laid them. I sat down at the desk and held his scriptures in my hands. When I unzipped the case and opened it, I found the note you just read serving as my son's bookmark. Gently laying the opened scriptures on the desk, I read the note. At the bottom of the last page, I saw a message from my son. I had not seen this message before. In that moment, it was like my son was with me again. Tears of joy ran down my cheeks as I saw in his handwriting the message, 'I love you, too, Daddy. I will always love you.'

"I read the words over and over. As I cherished these words from my son, a vision was opened to me. I was blessed to see the joyous reunion that occurred when Mikela was welcomed into the world of spirits with the warm embraces of family and friends who had gone before him. Mikela's entrance into the spirit world was a celebration, reminding me of the joy we experienced at his birth. After a period of greeting, welcoming, and celebration, I saw family and friends part and bow in reverence as Mikela was approached by a man whom I knew instantly. I was wrapped in the love of the Savior as I watched Him greet my son, saying, 'Mikela, welcome home.' He pulled Mikela tightly into his chest. Then He said, 'Well done, my good and faithful servant. Thou hast been faithful over a few things. I will make thee ruler over many things. Enter into the joy of your Lord.'

"My pain and sorrow were replaced with love and rejoicing. I knew my son was in the arms of his Savior and free from the pain, suffering, and anxieties of life. I knew he was happy and among family and friends. I rejoiced that my son had passed the test of mortality to be crowned with celestial glory.

"After the vision closed, I looked down and saw that the scriptures were open to John, chapter eleven. My eyes fixed on the famous two-word scripture, 'Jesus wept.' I read through the rest of the chapter, and the Lord ministered to me. While many have heard the famous scripture 'Jesus wept,' few are familiar with the circumstances that caused Jesus to weep. Jesus's friend, Lazarus became very sick, and Lazarus's sisters, Mary and Martha, sent for Jesus to come and be with Lazarus. When Jesus arrived, Lazarus had already been in the grave for four days, and many had gathered to comfort Mary and Martha with the loss of their brother."

Manu looked down at the scriptures in his hands and read, "Jesus saw [Mary] weeping, and he saw how the people with her were weeping also; his heart was touched, and he was deeply moved.[111] And said, Where have ye laid him? They said unto him, Lord, come and see. Jesus wept. Then said the Jews, 'Behold how He loved him!'[112]

"Jesus was deeply saddened by the death of His friend and came to mourn and cry with those who had gathered. A knowledge of the resurrection does not remove the pain of death or the mourning of those loved and lost. 'Mourning is one of the deepest expressions of pure love. It is a natural response in complete accord with the divine commandment: 'Thou shalt live together in love, insomuch that thou shalt weep for the loss of them that die.'[113]

"Jesus cried, even though He had a perfect knowledge of the resurrection and knew Lazarus would soon be raised from the dead.

For Jesus knows that 'we can't fully appreciate joyful reunions later without tearful separations now.'[114] Jesus came to weep and mourn with His friends. He also came to bring comfort, peace, and hope, declaring, 'I am the resurrection, and the life: he that believeth in me, though he were dead, yet shall he live.'[115] As I sat at my son's desk, the Savior came to weep with me as I mourned the loss of my son. He also came to comfort me, strengthen me, and to fill me with His peace and His love. He came to wipe the tears from my eyes.[116] Two weeks later, Elder Russel M. Nelson gave a talk at General Conference called 'Doors of Death.' It was as if he was speaking directly to me."

Manu pulled another paper from his scriptures and read us a portion of the talk by Elder Nelson: "'Recently at the funeral of a friend, I visited with two distinguished brothers—former surgical colleagues of mine—whose lovely companions had both passed away. They said they were going through the most difficult period of their lives, adjusting to the almost unbearable loss of their partners...Death...evokes pangs of sorrow and shock among those left behind. The hurt is real. Only its intensity varies. Some doors are heavier than others. The sense of tragedy may be related to age. Generally the younger the victim, the greater the grief...Life does not begin with birth, nor does it end with death. Prior to our birth, we dwelled as spirit children with our Father in Heaven. There we eagerly anticipated the possibility of coming to earth and obtaining a physical body. Knowingly we wanted the risks of mortality, which would allow the exercise of agency and accountability... We regarded the returning home as the best part of that long-awaited trip, just as we do now. Before embarking on any journey, we like to have some assurance of a round-trip ticket. Returning from earth to life in our heavenly home requires passage through—and not around—the doors of death. We were born to die, and we die to live.[117] As seedlings of God, we barely blossom on earth; we fully flower in Heaven... Our limited perspective would be enlarged if we could witness the reunion on the other side of the veil, when doors of death open to those returning home... As a special witness of Jesus Christ, I testify that He lives! I also testify that the veil of death is very thin. I know by experiences too sacred to relate that those who have gone before are not strangers to leaders of this Church. To us and to you, our loved ones may be just as close as the next room—separated only by the doors of death... With that assurance, brothers and sisters, love life! Cherish each moment as a blessing from God.'"[118]

Manu folded up the paper and placed it back into his scriptures. He smiled kindly as Elder Balane and I wiped at our eyes. "Cherish each moment, for we don't know when the door of death will open," he said. "Even as painful as death can be, you don't want to take the pain out of death. For 'the only way to take sorrow out of death is to take love out of life.'[119] Spend your time on that which is eternal so, when the door of death is open for you or for someone you love, there will be no fear, no despair, and no regrets."

CHAPTER 10

FINAL WEEK IN LĀNAʻI

"Let the mountains shout for joy, and all ye valleys cry aloud; and all ye seas and dry lands tell the wonders of your Eternal King! And ye rivers, and brooks, and rills, flow down with gladness. Let the woods and all the trees of the field praise the Lord; and ye solid rocks weep for joy! And let the sun, moon, and the morning stars sing together, and let all the sons of God shout for joy! And let the eternal creations declare his name forever and ever!"

- Doctrine and Covenants 128:23

It was Thursday evening and time for the call with transfer assignments. I'd only been in Lāna'i for a short three months, and I longed to continue my stay. Elder Balane had been on the island for five months, so I thought if either of us were getting transferred, it would be his time to go. When the phone rang, I answered.

"Elder Taylor, you are being transferred to Kapaa to serve as the zone leader of the Kaua'i zone," a firm male voice said.

I swallowed back my disappointment as I said the appropriate niceties and ended the call. I was sad I'd be leaving, but I felt the confirmation that this was the mind and will of the Lord. I called Brother Oshima, who was the counselor in the branch presidency on Lāna'i. He'd been in the branch presidency for decades, along with Brother Kawasaki. They'd each served as branch president several times, with the other serving as the counselor. They switched between being the president or counselor about every five years. Brother Oshima asked if I would speak that Sunday in Sacrament meeting. I was grateful for the opportunity to speak one last time to the faithful saints of Lānaʻi who were my family and friends.

That evening, before bed, and the following morning during my personal study, I began pondering and praying over the message the Lord would have me share. Sunday morning, I arose early to complete the talk. Around 8:45 a.m., Elder Balane and I departed our apartment and walked the few yards to the chapel next door for our 9:00 a.m. sacrament service.

Elder Balane surprised me by stopping me in the entrance of the meeting room and extending his hand. "It's been a pleasure serving with you," he said. "Let's keep in touch."

I nodded, touched at his sincerity, and followed him in.

Sister Kawasaki gave the opening prayer. As a part of her prayer, she prayed for the missionaries, mentioning Elder Balane and me by name. As she prayed for us, I was filled with the Spirit.

I was the last speaker on the program. I prayed mightily as we partook of the sacrament and as I listened to the speakers before me. I prayed for the gift of tongues that I might speak with the tongues of angels, which is to speak by the power of the Holy Ghost.

When it was my turn, I stood at the pulpit and opened with a hearty Aloha. The audience returned a warm Aloha. After a brief moment of silence to gather myself, I began:

I would like to thank you for your prayers. As Sister Kawasaki prayed for the missionaries, I was filled with the Spirit. It is such a blessing as a full-time missionary to have the faith and prayers of members throughout the world to lift us. I can feel your prayers—they strengthen me. Mahalo.

Our mission president has had us read Moroni, chapter seven, on charity every single day for the past year, and from you, I have seen and felt the pure love of Christ. I came here as a boy, and I hope to return home as a disciple.

I came here as a full-time missionary to share the good news of Jesus Christ, yet I have learned much more from you than you have learned from me. You have shown me what it looks like to live joyfully in Christ Jesus. I have seen "a more excellent way."[120] *I have been overwhelmed by your generosity and goodness. I have learned how to give and how to receive.*

I have learned that no matter the challenge or problem we face, Christ is the solution.

When you feel down, you can call on Jesus and He will lift you up.

When you feel weak, you can call on Jesus and He will make you strong.[121]

When you are in darkness or depressed, you can call on Jesus, the light and life of the world.[122]

When you are filled with anger, you can call on Jesus for the power to forgive.[123]

When you are weeping, you can call on Jesus. "For the Lamb... shall wipe away all tears."[124]

When you need strength, you can call on Jesus, who is the source of all power.[125]

When it seems the world has turned against you and you need a friend, you can call on Jesus, your perfect friend.[126]

When you are filled with guilt, you can call on Jesus who declares, "Be of good cheer, thy sins are forgiven thee."[127]

When you are filled with sorrow, you can call on Jesus and be filled with His peace.[128]

When you are afraid, you can call on Jesus for His unconditional love. "For perfect love casteth out all fear."[129]

When you have a question, you can call on Jesus, who is the fountain of all knowledge.[130]

During times of doubt, you can call on Jesus, saying, "Lord... help thou mine unbelief,"[131] *that He may give you the gift of faith to declare, "Lord, I believe."*[132]

The phrase "Ask and ye shall receive" is found over forty times in the scriptures. May we each recognize and call on Jesus and receive the great gifts He has for us. "For he that asketh, receiveth."[133]

I do sing and shout my praises to the great Jehovah, who will soon return in great glory, and close in the name of Jesus Christ, our Holy Messiah, the Prince of Peace, and our Perfect Friend. Amen.

The closing song was Aloha 'Oe (Farewell to Thee). It is a tradition in the islands to sing this song when someone is leaving. I joyfully listened to the beautiful Hawaiian voices as they sang to me.

The song has three verses with the chorus sung following each verse. The chorus and its translation are as follows:

Chorus
Aloha 'oe, aloha 'oe
E ke onaona noho i ka lipo
One fond embrace,
A ho'i a'e au
Until we meet again

English Translation
Farewell to thee, farewell to thee
The sweet and gentle one living for God
One fond embrace,
Before I now depart
Until we meet again

Tears streamed down my face. I felt the love of the Lāna'i branch as they sang for my farewell. I would miss these faithful saints. I was so overcome with emotion that I couldn't sing the final two verses of the song. Thankfully, I brought a recorder with me to preserve that moment. I've listened to that recording many times over the years, and each time I listen, I begin to cry as joyous memories fill my soul. Even though we're thousands of miles apart, as I listen, I feel connected to the warmth and love of these wonderful saints.

The closing prayer was offered, and the members of the branch and friends from the island of other denominations who had come to hear me speak stood in a line. Each greeted me with a hug, as well as a beautiful lei made from the island flowers. Manu was at the end of the line. He placed the final lei over my head and gave me his signature Hawaiian hug. As he lifted me off the ground, he said, "I will miss you, Elder Taylor. I love you."

At those words, I felt a peace, love, and warmth like never before during the past year and a half of hugs. The awkward sandpaper was gone. It felt as if the Savior Himself was giving me a hug. I was filled with the pure love of Christ. There are no words to adequately describe the feeling. I felt a trust and love for Manu that seemed to heal my soul. The parts of my heart closed by the pains of abuse were opened, and, for the first time, I could answer back without hesitation. "I love you, too, Manu. I love you, too!"

Manu set me on the ground and ended his loving embrace. "I'll see you tomorrow after school," he said. I was scheduled to take a ferry from Lāna'i to Maui early Monday night. From Maui I would take a flight to Kauai. I had one last visit with Manu.

Elder Balane and I spent the remainder of Sunday and our Monday P-day visiting the many friends we'd made. I wanted the chance to say good-bye to each of them personally before I left for Kaua'i. Monday afternoon came quickly, and we rode our bikes to the school to meet Manu.

"Where are you taking us today?" I asked Manu as we all climbed into his truck.

Manu smiled. "You'll see. As we drive, prepare yourself spiritually to receive."

As he pulled out of the school parking lot, Manu asked me a question. "Elder Taylor, do you make your bed each day?"

I thought this was a silly question but I answered, nonetheless. "No. I've never been one to make my bed. In fact, I can't remember the last time I made it. I'm just going to mess it up again in the evening, so what's the point?"

"Let me share with you a story," Manu answered in typical fashion. "A few years ago during summer break, I had the opportunity to take a week sabbatical to an isolated home in the mountains to work on a new book. With four children, there is rarely a quiet moment at home, so a week of isolation and quiet in the mountains was a change of pace. After I brought in my clothes, food, laptop, and boxes of books, I settled into a rocking chair in the living room. As I sat quietly in the chair, I had the impression that I needed to pray as I began the task of learning by revelation and writing by the Spirit.

"I began my prayer, and to my surprise, the prayer quickly turned into a dedicatory prayer. The Spirit took over and directed the words of my prayer. I stated the sacred name of Jesus Christ and exercised the Holy Priesthood to dedicate the home to be a Holy House of the Lord. I dedicated the home to be a place filled with the Spirit, filled with the presence of angels, filled with the presence of God the Father and His son Jesus Christ. I prayed for the angels to act as sentinels to protect against the forces of the adversary and to be messengers to bring the needed light, truth, direction, and wisdom that would be sought for and asked for throughout the week.

As I prayed, I could feel the transformation of the building into a mountain heiau (temple).

"The next morning, after I'd been reading for several hours, I took a break to walk through the home. As I moved through the rooms, I had the thought that angels were indeed there and the words of the dedicatory prayer from the previous night were brought to my mind. I was impressed with the feeling of peace that filled the home and how amazing it was to spend a week with the sounds of God's peace, creations, and angels, free from the distracting sounds of the world. I was impressed by the complete silence that permeated the home and the surrounding area. As I passed the bedroom, I noticed that the bed I'd slept in the night before was unmade. I had the subtle thought that I should make the bed. Like you, Elder Taylor, I was not one to make my bed. My first reaction was to continue walking down the hallway, but I quickly recognized that this quiet thought was not my own—it was the still, small voice of the Spirit. I went into the bedroom and made the bed to restore the order and cleanliness that should prevail in a house of the Lord. The rest of the home was very neat and orderly, with everything in its proper place. Elder Taylor, your home is to be a temple, correct?"

"I guess,'" I admitted.

"Do you think it's time you start making your bed?" Manu asked.

"I'd never viewed making my bed from this perspective," I said, not wanting to commit to a life a bed-making.

"So are you taking us to the island resort for one of the maids to teach us how to make beds?" Elder Balane asked with a smile.

Manu laughed. "No. I have one final story to share with you. I know the perfect place to share it. It's just ahead."

Moments later, Manu pulled off the side of the road. I got out of the car and looked around but didn't see any signs indicating where he was taking us. We followed Manu through thick brush and grasses. There was no trail and no sign of anyone else having come through this area.

Manu came to a full stop and then walked in a circular pattern, rounding a tree, passing by Elder Balane and me, and walking around another tree, all the while staring off into the distance with a small frown creasing his brow.

"Are we lost?" I asked after watching him wander.

"It's been several years since I've been to the place," Manu said. "Even the locals who have lived here for decades don't know about it. I think we're close."

Manu paused and bowed his head in prayer. Elder Balane and I waited in silence. Following his prayer, he looked around and began to walk up a hill to his left. We followed. Manu stopped in front of the opening of a small cave, satisfied. It was nestled into the side of the mountain, rock covered in moss, and the opening was so small, a person could easily walk by it if they weren't looking for it. The bright Hawaiian sun shone down, casting shadows at the entrance.

"Several summers ago, my wife and I were blessed with the opportunity to travel to Israel and visit the sites of the New Testament," he said, stepping toward the opening. "One of the highlights of the trip was our visit to the Garden Tomb where Jesus was laid, following

His crucifixion. I've brought you to this cave because it is surprisingly similar in size and appearance to the Garden Tomb.

"The New Testament gives accounts of Mary and Peter as they go into the Tomb on the first Easter morning. I wanted to see, as did Mary and Peter 'the place where the Lord lay.'[134] As I entered the Garden Tomb, I beheld in a vision the tomb on that glorious Sunday morning. After the resurrection, Jesus did not leave his bed unmade.[135] As I entered the sacred tomb, I saw in vision neatly folded burial clothes and coverings, and I heard the words of an angel speaking to me, 'He is not here. He is risen!'"[136]

Tears flowed down Manu's cheeks as he shared the words of the angel. We stood quietly in profound gratitude, overwhelmed by the goodness of the Lord Jesus.

"When I exited the tomb," Manu continued, "my eyes were drawn toward Heaven, and I gazed into the beautiful sky above. With my face turned toward Heaven, I spoke these words to Jesus: 'Thank you! Thank you! I love you!' As I spoke these words, I was wrapped with a love that is impossible for words to fully describe. Then I heard the voice of the Lord say to me, 'I love you, too. I love you, too.'"

We basked in the Spirit and love of the resurrected Lord as we each took our turn entering the cave and reliving the experience of those who came to the tomb on that first Easter morning. No words were spoken and no words were needed because we were taught directly by the Spirit. Although it seemed like we were there for a brief moment, in reality, much time had passed.

After each of us had spent time in the cave, Manu broke the

silence. "I wish we could stay longer, but it is time to get you home so Elder Taylor can catch the ferry."

Manu drove back to the school to drop me off for the last time.

"I have one last lesson in the Hawaiian language," Manu said as we put on our helmets and unlocked our bikes. "As you know, Aloha has many, many meanings. In recent history, it's often said that Aloha can be used for hello and good-bye. However, in the original Hawaiian language and culture, there were no good-byes. The concept of separation or relationships ending does not exist in the original language. Once a connection was made, it was believed that the connection remained into eternity. Elder Taylor, our friendship is eternal. There is no end. There are no good-byes. We will always be connected, even if we're not in the same physical location. The closest thing to good-bye in Hawaiian is 'a hui ho' which means 'until we meet again.'"

A wide smile stretched across Manu's face as he clapped me on the back and said in his joyful Hawaiian way, "A hui ho, Elder Taylor, a hui ho."

Manu's joyful nature and his spirit-filled "a hui ho" returned a smile to my face. With as much joy as I could muster, I replied, "A hui ho, Manu. A hui ho."

I stood beside Elder Balane, straddling my bike. I watched my dear friend drive away and my heart felt heavy. Although I knew we would meet again, I was very sad to be leaving. I blinked at the tears now filling my eyes and whispered, "Until we meet again. Until we meet again."

Epilogue

This is the first book in *The Way of Aloha* series. Future books will take place on other Hawaiian islands, where we will visit historical and sacred locations on these islands and explore additional truths and principles from ancient Hawai'i. Future books in the series will include:

The Way of Aloha: Moloka'i
The Way of Aloha: Maui
The Way of Aloha: The Big Island
The Way of Aloha: O'ahu
The Way of Aloha: Kaua'i

Acknowledgments

I would like to thank the many people who helped with the completion of this book. I would like to express individual thanks:

To Paula Taylor. I am greatly blessed to be married to Paula. She is a woman of many, many talents. She has played a key role in the writing and editing of each of my books. I appreciate her constant and enduring support.

To Todd Thompson for the cover art and book design—he is a brilliant designer who is fantastic to work with.

To Janis Bowers. She is a gifted editor. She has an eye for detail and caught many mistakes missed by other editors. Mahalo for your service.

To William Croyle, Crystal Liechty, Heather Moore, Amanda Brown, and Stephanie Clarke for their work as editors.

About the Author

Cameron C. Taylor is a best-selling author, highly sought-after speaker, and entrepreneur. Cameron is the author of the books *Preserve, Protect, and Defend*; *Does Your Bag Have Holes? 24 Truths That Lead to Financial and Spiritual Freedom*; *8 Attributes of Great Achievers*; and *Twelve Paradoxes of the Gospel.* Cameron graduated with honors from Brigham Young University Marriott School of Management and is the founder of several successful companies and charities. He is a founder of The Glorious Cause of America Institute and serves on its board of directors. Cameron is a recipient of the Circle of Honor Award for being an "exceptional example of honor, integrity, and commitment." He lives in Idaho with his wife and children. Cameron is a gifted teacher who has been invited to speak at hundreds of meetings with excellent reviews.

Cameron's books and lectures have been endorsed by Ken Blanchard, co-author of *The One Minute Manager*; Dr. Stephen R. Covey, author of *The Seven Habits of Highly Effective People*; Billionaire Jon Huntsman, Sr.; Rich DeVos, owner of the Orlando Magic; William Danko, PhD, co-author of *The Millionaire Next Door*; and many others.

Aloha@CameronCTaylor.com

www.CameronCTaylor.com

Endnotes

1 Statement by Howard W. Hunter at 1994 Hawai'i Honolulu Mission Training.
2 *Hymns* (Salt Lake City: The Church of Jesus Christ of Latter-day Saints, 1985), 270.
3 Thomas Paine, *The Works of Thomas Paine, Volume 1* (Philadelphia: James Carey, 1797), 53.
4 David O. McKay, Clare Middlemiss, *Cherished Experiences from the Writings of President David O. McKay* (Salt Lake City, UT: Deseret Book, 1955), 101-102.
5 Joseph Smith, Jr., Joseph Fielding Smith, *Teachings of the Prophet Joseph Smith* (Salt Lake City, UT: Deseret Book, 1976), 191.
6 Doctrine and Covenants 109:7.
7 George Sylvester Viereck, *Glimpses of the Great* (London: Duckworth, 1930), 364.
8 Alma 30:44.
9 Spencer W. Kimball, "Continuous Revelation," General Conference, October 1966.
10 Mark 4:9.
11 Matthew 13:16.
12 Doctrine and Covenants 76:10.
13 Ezekiel 12:2.
14 Moses 7:18.
15 John H. Groberg, *In the Eye of the Storm* (Salt Lake City: Bookcraft, 1993), 175.
16 1 Corinthians 12:31.
17 John 10:10.
18 Acts 4:32, 34, New International Version (NIV).
19 Acts 4:32, New International Version (NIV).
20 George Q. Cannon, Jerreld L. Newquist, *Gospel Truth: Discourses and Writings of George Q. Cannon* (Salt Lake City: Deseret Book, 1987), 525.
21 Matthew 6:19.
22 Isaiah 11:1, Isaiah 53:2.
23 John 15:1-6.
24 Matthew 22:37-39.
25 Matthew 7:12.
26 Matthew 25:40.
27 John Taylor, "The Organization of the Church," *Millennial Star*, Nov. 15, 1851, p. 339.
28 Brigham Young, *Deseret News: Semi-Weekly*, June 7, 1870, p. 3.
29 Stephen E. Robinson, *Following Christ* (Salt Lake City: Deseret Book, 1995), 129-130.
30 Matthew 5:20.
31 Exodus 20:13.

32 Doctrine and Covenants 58:27-29.

33 Harrington Emerson, American efficiency engineer. Quoted in Gilbert P. Farrar, *The Typography of Advertisements that Pay* (New York: D. Appleton and Company, 1920), title page.

34 John 4:32, 34.

35 Neil L. Andersen, "Repent...That I May Heal You," *General Conference*, October 2009.

36 Charles W. Kenn, "What is a Haole?" *Paradise of the Pacific,* August 1944, p. 16.

37 Madeleine L'Engle, *Walking on Water* (New York: North Point Press, 1980), 181–182.

38 Exodus 3:5.

39 Psalm 46:10.

40 Matthew 9:2.

41 Matthew 18:20.

42 Matthew 9:2, 6.

43 Matthew 11:28-30.

44 Numbers 21:6-9.

45 1 Nephi 17:41, Alma 33:20.

46 Isaiah 1:18; Jeremiah 31:34.

47 Doctrine and Covenants 58:42.

48 1 John 1:7-9.

49 Matthew 9:2.

50 Doctrine and Covenants 19:16, 18.

51 1 Nephi 22:4.

52 William "Pila" Chiles, *The Secrets & Mysteries of Hawaii* (Deerfield Beach, FL: Health Communication, 1995), 205.

53 1 Nephi 21:15-16.

54 John 16:23-24, New King James Version (NKJV).

55 *Bible Dictionary*, "Prayer," p. 752-753.

56 Akiane and Foreli Kramarik, *Akiane: Her Life, Her Art, Her Poetry* (Nashville, TN: W Publishing Group, 2006), 12.

57 James 4:2.

58 Romans 8:26.

59 James 4:3.

60 Matthew 17:14–21.

61 Richard Lyman Bushman, *Joseph Smith: Rough Stone Rolling* (New York: Random House, 2005), 73.

62 Doctrine and Covenants 9:7-10.

63 Joseph Fielding Smith, *Doctrines of Salvation, Volume 3* (Salt Lake City: Bookcraft, 1956), 216.

64 Joseph had the plates for two hundred and two days before the first page was translated. During this time he worked on developing his gift and tried various approaches but only translated a few figures and characters. The translation of the book of Lehi began on April 12, 1828 and took sixty-four days to translate

one hundred and sixteen written pages. The book of Lehi was translated at an average rate of 1.81 pages per day. With the loss of the book of Lehi, Joseph's gift to translate was taken from him for a season. The translation work was resumed with Oliver Cowdery as Joseph's scribe on April 7, 1829. They began the translation of the portions of the gold plates we have today as the Book of Mormon. It took eighty-five days to translate four hundred and sixty-six written pages. This translation was done at a rate of 5.48 pages per day—over three times faster than the first one hundred sixteen pages. The increase in Joseph's translation speed is an illustration of this truth: "That which we persist in doing becomes easier for us to do; not that the nature of the thing itself is changed, but that our power to do is increased." (Ralph Waldo Emerson quoted by President Heber J. Grant. "Seventieth Annual Conference of the Church of Jesus Christ of Latter-day Saints," *The Deseret News,* 1900, p. 63)

65 Richard Lyman Bushman, *Joseph Smith: Rough Stone Rolling* (New York: Random House, 2005), 63–64.

66 *Bible Dictionary*, "Prayer," p. 753.

67 John 4:10, New Living Translation (NLT).

68 Matthew 7:7.

69 Doctrine and Covenants 88:29-31. "Ye who are quickened by a portion of the celestial glory shall then receive of the same, even a fulness. And they who are quickened by a portion of the terrestrial glory shall then receive of the same, even a fulness. And also they who are quickened by a portion of the telestial glory shall then receive of the same, even a fulness."

70 Doctrine and Covenants 88:32-33.

71 Psalm 23:5.

72 David Noel Freedman, *The Anchor Bible Dictionary, Volume 6* (New York: Double Day, 1992), 907.

Walter A. Elwell, *Baker Encyclopedia of the Bible, Volume 1* (Grand Rapids, MI: Baker Book House, 1988), 491. During the time of the New Testament, a talent was approximately 750 ounces of silver. A pence was approximately 1/8 of an ounce of silver. Thus, one talent equaled 6,000 pence (750 divided by 1/8). One pence was the day wage of a laborer. To calculate today's dollar value equivalents, I estimated the wage of a laborer at $50 per day ($6.25/hour for 8 hours) and multiplied that by the number of pence. Thus, one talent in the New Testament is equal to $300,000 in US currency (6,000 multiplied by $50).

73 Matthew 25:21.

74 Matthew 25:26.

75 Matthew 25:29.

76 Jacob 2:18-19.

77 Acts 20:35.

78 Acts 20:35, Contemporary English Version (CEV).

79 Luke 10:30-35.

80 Hyrum L. Andrus and Helen Mae Andrus, *They Knew the Prophet* (Salt Lake City: Bookcraft, 1974), 146.

81 *Teachings of Presidents of the Church: Spencer W. Kimball* (Salt Lake City: The Church of Jesus Christ of Latter-day Saints, 2006), 103.

82 Alan L. Chisholm, "Coping with Envy," *Psychotherapy & Spirituality Institute*, retrieved January 11, 2007, from http://www.mindspirit.org/psiqa04.htm.

83 Acts 7:9.

84 Richard Paul Evans, *The Four Doors: A Guide to Joy, Freedom, and a Meaningful Life* (New York: Simon & Schuster, 2013), 40-42.

85 Ezra Taft Benson, "Beware of Pride," General Conference, April 1989.

86 Stephen R. Covey, *Principle-Centered Leadership* (New York: Simon & Schuster, 1991), 159.

87 I had this dream on December 25, 2014. The details of the dream and interpretation of the dream have not been changed or adapted other than having the dream told by the character Manu.

88 2 Nephi 2:27.

89 *Bible Dictionary*, "War in Heaven," p. 788.

90 Doctrine and Covenants 76:25-26.

91 Isaiah 5:20.

92 Matthew 24:24.

93 *Teachings of Presidents of the Church: Joseph Fielding Smith* (Salt Lake City: The Church of Jesus Christ of Latter-day Saints, 2013), 143.

94 Hyrum W. Smith, *The Ten Natural Laws of Successful Time and Life Management* (New York: Warner Books, 1994), 147.

95 Boyd K. Packer, *Conference Report*, October 1986, p. 20.

96 Poll results retrieved from http://www.gallup.com/poll/161987/hawaii-remains-state-least-stress.aspx.

97 Doctrine and Covenants 38:2.

98 2 Nephi 2:25.

99 Matthew 6:34.

100 Matthew 6:34, Living Bible (TLB).

101 This experience is taken from my journal written while I was at a cabin in Island Park, Idaho working on this book. I had the dream on December 15, 2014. The details of the story and the dream have not been changed or adapted other than having the dream told by the character Manu.

102 Hebrews 13:5, New King James Version (NKJV).

103 Philippians 3:13-14.

104 Lamentations 3:21-23, Good News Translation (GNT).

105 Matthew 9:2, Mark 2:5.

106 Luke 19:9-10.

107 Doctrine and Covenants 1:31.

108 Bruce R. McConkie, "The Probationary Test of Mortality," Address given at University of Utah Institute, Jan. 10, 1982, p. 11.

109 Moroni 10:32-33, Colossians 1:28.

110 Thomas S. Monson, "The Holy Temple—A Beacon to the World," General Conference, April 2011.

111 John 11:33, Good News Translation.

112 John 11:34-36.
113 Doctrine and Covenants 42:45.
114 Russel M. Nelson, "Doors of Death," General Conference, April 1992.
115 John 11:25.
116 "For the Lamb...shall wipe away all tears from their eyes." Revelations 7:17.
117 See 2 Corinthians 6:9.
118 Russel M. Nelson, "Doors of Death," General Conference, April 1992.
119 Russel M. Nelson, "Doors of Death," General Conference, April 1992.
120 1 Corinthians 12:31.
121 Ether 12:27.
122 3 Nephi 9:18.
123 Mark 2:10.
124 Revelations 7:17.
125 Matthew 28:18.
126 Doctrine and Covenants 84:77.
127 Matthew 9:2.
128 John 14:27.
129 Moroni 8:16.
130 Daniel 2:19-20. "George A. Smith, while serving in the First Presidency, stated: 'Joseph Smith taught that every man and woman should seek the Lord for wisdom, that they might get knowledge from Him who is the fountain of knowledge; and the promises of the gospel, as revealed, were such as to authorize us to believe, that by taking this course we should gain the object of our pursuit.'" (*Teachings of Presidents of the Church: Joseph Smith* (Salt Lake City: The Church of Jesus Christ of Latter-day Saints, 2007), 266).
131 Mark 9:24.
132 John 9:38.
133 3 Nephi 27:29.
134 Matthew 28:6.
135 John 20:6-7, Holman Christian Standard Bible. "Simon Peter came also. He entered the tomb and saw the linen cloths lying there. The wrapping that had been on His head was not lying with the linen cloths but was folded up in a separate place by itself."
Eldred G. Smith, "Three Days in the Tomb," *General Conference*, April 1974. "Mary found and told Peter and John. They came running. John, the younger, arrived first, looked in the tomb, but did not enter until after Peter had entered. The body was gone, but the linens were there, neatly folded."
136 Mathew 28:6.

8 Attributes of Great Achievers

"I thought *8 Attributes of Great Achievers* was an excellent read with interesting and deep stories. I enjoyed it more than any book I've read in quite a while. I had a hard time putting it down."

-Mark Dennison

Twelve Paradoxes of the Gospel

"Cameron's strong faith comes through in his book and there is no doubt he was inspired to write it."

-Lou Holtz, Former Head Football Coach, *University of Notre Dame*

Preserve, Protect & Defend

"*Preserve, Protect & Defend* was a great read, filled with the spirit all through. No man wrote it, God did. I'm 61 and cried all through it. Thank you for sharing your talents."

-S. Dean Chappell

8 Attributes of Great Achievers Volume II

"I am writing to share with you how much I enjoyed reading your book. I was deeply touched, encouraged, inspired, and challenged. I laughed and I cried. Every day I have been sharing with my husband what I am learning, and I keep on saying 'This is such an amazing book!!!'"

-Cora Bushey

8 Steps to Lasting Excellence

"Phenomenal. I devoured this book in 3 days, as the stories, lessons, and insights proved amazing."

-Christopher Wild

Does Your Bag Have Holes?

"Cameron was meant to write, and he does so beautifully. He writes with humor, insight, and profound wisdom. I came across so many different stories that I wanted to scan/type in and share. They're that amazing."

-Joi Sigers

Available at: www.CameronCTaylor.com